THE MEANING OF OTHER FAITHS

LIBRARY OF LIVING FAITH

JOHN M MULDER, General Editor

THE MEANING
OF
OTHER FAITHS

By

WILLARD G. OXTOBY

With a Preface by
HANS KÜNG

THE WESTMINSTER PRESS
PHILADELPHIA

BOOK DESIGN BY DOROTHY ALDEN SMITH

First edition

Published by The Westminster Press®
Philadelphia, Pennsylvania

PRINTED IN THE UNITED STATES OF AMERICA
9 8 7 6 5 4 3 2 1

Library of Congress Cataloging in Publication Data

Oxtoby, Willard Gurdon.
  The meaning of other faiths.

  (Library of living faith)
  Bibliography: p.
  1. Christianity and other religions. I. Title.
II. Series.
BR127.O87 1983   261.2   83-1090
ISBN 0-664-24443-2 (pbk.)

CONTENTS

ACKNOWLEDGMENTS

I owe the main impetus for this book to the Ecumenical
Forum of Canada. Under its sponsorship in 1980 I con-
vened a study group on the Christian understanding of
religions, and met periodically with nine Toronto col-
leagues. They were Anglicans Michael Marmura, Oliver
O'Donovan, and Cyril Powles; Roman Catholics Julia
Ching, Thomas Langan, Harry McSorley, and Kenneth
Schmitz; and from the United Church of Canada Heinz
Guenther and Douglas Jay. We planned eventually to
produce a jointly written document; something may yet
develop, given time. With the invitation from The Westminster Press to contribute to the Library of Living Faith, I
ventured forth on my own. A research leave in 1981–82 in
Australia, China, India, and the Middle East provided
opportunities for reflection.

For years of encouragement on historical, comparative,
and theological topics I am indebted to Charles Adams and
Stanley Frost at McGill, Norvin Hein at Yale, Edward Jurji
at Princeton Seminary, Joseph Kitagawa at Chicago, John
Marks at Princeton University, and Wilfred Smith at Harvard. Many others whom I have come to know more
recently, including adherents of each major religious tradition, living in the West and in Asia, have also contributed
much to the shaping of my perceptions. No one but myself,

8   ACKNOWLEDGMENTS

however, is accountable for the sins of omission and of commission which afflict this little book.

This book is dedicated to the memory of Layla Oxtoby (1935–1980), whose courage and whose encouragement were something very special indeed.

W.G.O.

PREFACE

"Why study other religions?" ask conservative Christians, unwilling to question their own faith. "What's the use?" echo the skeptical secularists, holding religion irrelevant to happiness.

The fact is: modern faith in science, technology, and progress—our surrogate gods—has been shaken. And humanity's faith in the transcendent dimension in life and history, in spite of everything, has persisted and shown itself remarkably resilient.

Yet humanity lives without peace, threatened with its own destruction, while religious or quasi-religious conflicts lead often to political and military confrontations: between Hindus and Muslims in India and Pakistan, Shi'is and Sunnis in Iran and Iraq, and the communities in the Middle East and in northern Ireland. More and more the religion question has become the peace question. And so:

1. Only if we seek to understand others'—our neighbors'—beliefs and values, rites and symbols, can we truly understand other people.

2. Only if we seek to understand others' faith can we really understand our own: its strengths and weaknesses, its constants and variables.

3. Only if we seek to understand others' faith can we discover that common ground which, despite all differences, can become the basis for a peaceful life in this world together.

9

To become acquainted with the meaning of others' faith is a long and tedious process. Look how long it took Protestants to discover one another, and then to understand Catholics and be understood in return. The dialogue of Christians with Jews, Muslims, and even with Hindus, Buddhists, Confucians, and Taoists, will take more time and patience. But it is not hopeless, as experience of it confirms. In spite of wars and catastrophes, the twentieth century is marked by the earnestness and scholarly preparations with which dialogue between Christianity and other religions has been undertaken.

Professor Willard G. Oxtoby's book comes at just the right time. Here the reader finds in compact form: (a) that the Bible itself contains various stances toward other religions; (b) what the Christian church's often ambivalent stance was toward Jews, Muslims, and "pagans"; (c) how today this stance, and even the Christian "mission," must be rethought; (d) how interreligious dialogues were formerly conducted and how they should proceed today; and finally (e) how the very difficult question of truth claims may be tackled.

Some of this book's theses, especially regarding religious truth, will provoke discussion. But bear in mind that the author (1) knows other religions not only from books but also from life, (2) addresses not only the current problem but also the long, complex history of the religions and their relationships to one another; and (3) has mastered vast material and presented it in an intelligible manner.

The book's exemplary balance, measured judgment, and optimistic pointing of the way forward come from a scholar who confesses himself a Christian and reveals the greatest openness toward all non-Christians. The book makes it crystal clear: after intra-Protestant and intra-Christian ecumenism we have irrevocably reached the third ecumenical dimension, ecumenism of the world religions!

HANS KÜNG

University of Tübingen
October 1982

FOREWORD

The word "theology" comes from two Greek words—*theos* ("God") and *logos* ("word" or "thought"). Theology is simply words about God or thinking about God. But for many Christians, theology is remote, abstract, baffling, confusing, and boring. They turn it over to the professionals—the theologians—who can ponder and inquire into the ways of God with the world.

This series, Library of Living Faith, is for those Christians who thought theology wasn't for them. It is a collection of ten books on crucial doctrines or issues in the Christian faith today. Each book attempts to show why our theology—our thoughts about God—matters in what we do and say as Christians. The series is an invitation to readers to become theologians themselves—to reflect on the Bible and on the history of the church and to find their own ways of understanding the grace of God in Jesus Christ.

The Library of Living Faith is in the tradition of another series published by Westminster Press in the 1950s, the Layman's Theological Library. This new collection of volumes tries to serve the church in the challenges of the closing decades of this century.

The ten books are based on the affirmation of the Letter to the Ephesians (4:4–6): "There is one body and one Spirit, just as you were called to the one hope that belongs to your call, one Lord, one faith, one baptism, one God and

11

Father of us all, who is above all and through all and in all."
Each book addresses a particular theme as part of the
Christian faith as a whole; each book speaks to the church
as a whole. Theology is too important to be left only to the
theologians; it is the work and witness of the entire people
of God.

But, as Ephesians says, "grace was given to each of us
according to the measure of Christ's gift" (Eph. 4:7), and
the Library of Living Faith tries to demonstrate the diversity of theology in the church today. Differences, of course,
are not unique to American Christianity. One only needs to
look at the New Testament and the early church to see how
"the measure of Christ's gift" produced disagreement and
conflict as well as a rich variety of understandings of
Christian faith and discipleship. In the midst of the unity of
the faith, there has never been uniformity. The authors in
this series have their own points of view, and readers may
argue along the way with the authors' interpretations. But
each book presents varying points of view and shows what
difference it makes to take a particular theological position.
Sparks may fly, but the result, we hope, will be a renewed
vision of what it means to be a Christian exhibiting in the
world today a living faith.

These books are also intended to be a library—a set of
books that should be read together. Of course, not everything is included. As the Gospel of John puts it, "There are
also many other things which Jesus did; were every one of
them to be written I suppose that the world itself could not
contain the books that would be written" (John 21:25).
Readers should not be content to read just the volume on
Jesus Christ or on God or on the Holy Spirit and leave out
those on the church or on the Christian life or on Christianity's relationship with other faiths. For we are called to one
faith with many parts.

The volumes are also designed to be read by groups of
people. Writing may be a lonely task, but the literature of
the church was never intended for individuals alone. It is

for the entire body of Christ. Through discussion and even
debate, the outlines of a living faith can emerge.

This book deals with an ancient question, as old as
Israel's confrontation with the gods of their neighbors, as
old as Paul's sermon on Mars' Hill. And yet, as Willard
Oxtoby argues, the relationship between Christianity and
other faiths has become an urgent question in our modern
world. It is a question as immediate as the multiplicity of
religious groups in America today, and it affects every
Christian in dealing with both other Christians and people
who are not Christian. It is also a question that goes beyond
personal relationships, for in the world today, religion
continues to shape social, economic, and political relationships between peoples and nations.

Willard Oxtoby comes to this study as a specialist in
comparative religions. An ordained minister in The United
Presbyterian Church in the U.S.A., he is Professor of
Religious Studies at the University of Toronto, and he has
written extensively on pre-Islamic religions and religious
ideas. He holds degrees from Stanford University in philosophy and humanities and from Princeton University in
Near Eastern languages. He has taught at McGill University, the University of Michigan, Harvard, and Yale; and has
done postgraduate research at the Harvard University Center for the Study of World Religions and the American
Schools of Oriental Research.

JOHN M. MULDER

Louisville Presbyterian Theological Seminary
Louisville, Kentucky

INTRODUCTION / The Problem Stated

The task of our inquiry may be put simply: to explore the meaning of the diversity of religions for Christians today. We cannot afford to be ignorant of the world's great traditions, and we cannot avoid contact with their adherents. Yet as Christians we have been taught that ours is the full, final, and definitive revelation of the one God. If we are to be true to our own faith, what basis is there for any appreciation of the faith of others?

The spectrum of answers to such a question is certainly broad. Christian estimates of other religions have ranged all the way from what one might call a "benighted heathen" view to a "many paths up the mountain" view. Under the first of these, Christianity is the one and only truth, utterly different from other religions or at least significantly different insofar as it is the only path to salvation. Under the second, Christianity is one of the religions, all of which in their various ways lead people to God, and therefore presumably similar to other religions rather than different from them precisely on the point of being a path to salvation and a channel of God's grace.

Between such polar opposites, what are we as individual Christians to do? What does the tradition of our Christian community teach? What factual information about religions do we need to consider? And on what points of evaluation or interpretation do we need to make an individual commitment?

To answer these questions I will look at the sources and development of Christian tradition. Then I will examine the nature of our involvement with the world's religions, and discuss the principles of communication, comparison, and evaluation for interreligious encounter. Each of these topics is rich both in data and in theoretical interpretation. Our seemingly simple agenda turns out to be more involved but also rewarding. As we shall see, the basic issue is still "up for grabs." Christians *do* differ as to their evaluation of other religions. The discussion is wide open; indeed, it is the most important unresolved theological question of our times. How we decide, and the reasoning by which we make our decisions, may have an important part in shaping the future of the Christian tradition itself.

1
STARTING WITH THE BIBLE

For many Christians the Bible is the chief and classic source of religious authority, but within the Bible there are a variety of perceptions of other peoples and their gods, and a range of interpretation of their significance to Israel and to the church. This range includes views of other nations as threats to God's plan and as instruments of it; and it includes views of the piety of others as spurious and as genuine. Consider a few examples of this diversity.

THE HEBREW KINGDOMS

The court of King Solomon in the tenth century B.C. was a splendid affair, in the thinking of an ancient Hebrew. Formerly obscure, the Hebrew tribes had quickly been catapulted into the position of a significant regional power. It was new, and noteworthy, that a neighboring queen from the realm of Sheba should come to pay respects. The Hebrews were proud that Solomon could import materials and workmen from Phoenicia to build an impressive temple to the Lord in Jerusalem. A more debatable point is whether Solomon was as wise as he was reputed to be. Many of the splendors of his reign were built through the conscription of labor. They left behind a resentment of the central government in Jerusalem which erupted in the secession of the ten northern tribes on Solomon's death.

Like other rulers of his day, Solomon entered into political marriages with princesses of neighboring kingdoms, and he built altars in Jerusalem for his many wives. If a Hittite princess was to live in Solomon's palace, then the Hittite religion had to be present there. If Syrian and Aramean wives were to take up residence in the palace, then they too would bring the images and the paraphernalia of their gods with them. One interpretation to be drawn from this state of affairs is that for the Hebrew monarchy at the peak of its power, Yahweh was the God of Israel and of its fortunes, but the worship of other gods was deemed appropriate, at least for politically significant aliens living within Yahweh's territory. Other gods were real and legitimate for people other than the Israelites. The command, "You shall have no other gods before me," was addressed principally to the Israelites.

One of the most dramatic episodes in the Old Testament is the narrative of the confrontation of the Hebrew prophet Elijah with the priests of the Canaanite and Phoenician god Baal in the eighth century B.C. The Bible presents the narrative not as a question of whether both Hebrew and Canaanite gods exist, but as a question of which god is sovereign in the land of the Israelites. The sovereignty is, in the end, exclusively Yahweh's.

The terms of the contest are set in the context of a drought which has parched the countryside. The priests of Baal first engage in their rituals, calling on Baal to bring rain. Since he is known in Canaanite literature as the rider of the clouds, we can expect Baal to be particularly generous in things meteorological. But to no avail. Following the Baal priests' efforts, not a cloud is in sight.

Next it is Elijah's turn to call on Yahweh. Elijah puts the matter almost as a matter of pride: let Yahweh show that he is lord in this land. And from Mt. Carmel all who are present look toward the Mediterranean to the west, and a tiny cloud appears which then grows into a mighty rain-

storm and vindicates the care of Yahweh for his land. The
Lord is sovereign on Mt. Carmel. Baal, however powerful
he may be farther north, has no place in Israel's territory.

The Old Testament prophets whose words come down to
us in written collections include Isaiah, who lived through
the fall of the northern Israelite kingdom to the Assyrians in
722 B.C.; and Jeremiah, who lived through the fall of the
southern kingdom, Judah, to the Babylonians in 587 B.C. In
the prophetic books, one can detect a recurrent effort to
interpret current events in the light of a reward-and-punish-
ment theology of national morality. For most of the prophets, prosperity or at least survival would be the reward of a
faithful people who maintained a righteous society, whereas destruction and ruin lay in store for those who ignored
Yahweh and his commands for justice.

It is probably safe to say that the prophets' concern was
largely with the faithfulness and righteousness of the Israelites. It was the Hebrews, and not the Edomites or
Phoenicians or Assyrians, who were supposed to follow the
commandments of Yahweh; and it was Israelite unfaithful-
ness which in the prophets' views Yahweh saw fit to
punish. To this end, Yahweh was seen as *using* foreign
nations to implement his agenda for Israel. The Assyrians
and other nations could be the "rod of Yahweh's anger," by
which blows could be meted out to Israel. And if the
Assyrian campaign against Jerusalem was withdrawn because "the angel of Yahweh slew 185,000 in the camp of the
Assyrians," i.e., because of an outbreak of disease in Senna-
cherib's army, the Hebrews saw it not as a judgment on the
Assyrians but as a reprieve for Jerusalem. Only in a few
instances do prophetic oracles against foreign nations casti-
gate those nations for exceeding the punitive role decreed
for them in God's plan for the people of ancient Israel.

A watershed figure in the development of the religious
thought of the Old Testament was the anonymous sixth-
century B.C. writer in the prophetic tradition whose words

have been included in the Book of Isaiah as chapters 40 through 55. Since he was identified as a separate writer by nineteenth-century scholars, he has been known as "Second Isaiah." Second Isaiah apparently lived in Babylon around 540 B.C., toward the end of the Babylonian exile. More than three decades earlier the Babylonians had conquered Palestine, destroyed the Jerusalem Temple, and deported the Judean intelligentsia as captives. Now Babylon's power was ebbing, and the Persians to the east were going from one victory to another, threatening to sweep all before them.

In chapter 45, Second Isaiah holds out some rather remarkable expectations for Cyrus, the Persian king. In Isaiah's words, Cyrus is the Lord's kingly ruler or messiah—i.e., "anointed one," for the use of ointment was a ritual sign of kingship in the ancient Near East. Cyrus is going to break down gates and open doorways—presumably, to conquer Babylon—so that people may know from east to west that Yahweh is God. Yahweh gives Cyrus his name, though Cyrus does not know it. Yahweh establishes good and evil. Yahweh, in sum, is now undisputed lord of the whole universe. No longer is his territory limited to Palestine; now he is lord of all the known world, and the goal is that everyone shall acknowledge his lordship.

This cosmic sovereignty is expressed in other, less political terms in Isaiah 40. There, God creates the heavens as well as the earth, and is not to be compared to the vain, impotent idols of others. By an almost inevitable progression, the God who had tolerated the cults of alien wives in Solomon's day had confirmed his sole dominion over the land of the Israelites in Elijah's, had used other nations to bring about his will for Israel in Jeremiah's, and was ruling other nations, however anonymously, for their own sakes in Second Isaiah's.

In the period of the Babylonian exile, what became Judaism emerged from the state cult of the shattered

Hebrew kingdom. Urban as well as agrarian, Aramaic as well as Hebrew, priestly instead of monarchical, Judaism—became an international religion. It had the potential of existing under alien rule and in scattered lands, even as it yearned for a restoration of the Davidic monarchy.

Judaism had the potential of incorporating aliens into its community. On this point it is clear that there was a tension between inclusivists and exclusivists. "Third Isaiah" (chapters 56 to 66), writing about 515 B.C., holds that foreigners and eunuchs are welcome among God's people, despite what some may say, for God will accept all who keep his sabbaths. The Book of Ruth narrates how a woman from Moab could be accepted into the community of the Israelites, and even makes Ruth an ancestor of King David. The Book of Jonah is a little narrative masterpiece. Its point is not whether someone can survive being swallowed by a fish; the fish is there, after Jonah has taken a ship in the opposite direction, simply to get him back on land to face his prophetic mission. The book's point is that Jonah is supposed to preach to the Assyrians. The Assyrians, much to Jonah's surprise, actually repent, and then Jonah sulks, begrudging their repentance. In response, Yahweh asks the culminating question: "Don't you think I care about Nineveh?"

So the conception that the God of Israel is not only all-powerful but cares for the world (whether "the world" knows it or not) develops during the course of ancient Israel's religious history and remains as one of the teachings of Scripture.

Along with the development of the scope of God's power goes a development in the awareness of human obligation. In its simplest terms, this has been expressed by modern interpreters as a development from a ritual to a moral sense. The Hebrews, they say, originally had certain agricultural festivals that followed the succession of the seasons, an observance of rest from work on the Sabbath, and a strict

and complex set of dietary restrictions. Under the influence
of the prophets, the emphasis was shifted to a concern first
and foremost for righteousness and justice. Isaiah 1:11 has
been cited in this antiritualist interpretation as a repudiation of ceremony in favor of morality. The prophet says on
God's behalf, "I cannot endure iniquity and solemn assembly" (v. 13). But there is an equally plausible interpretation.
Isaiah's outburst is a denunciation not of ritual as such but
of hypocrisy in ritual. Ritual, far from being an abomination
to God, should be a symbol of a right state of affairs between
God and humanity. The Lord is sick of the sacrifices
because of the people's iniquity and not because he has
anything against sacrifices as such.

This conflict in interpretation relates to the question of
universalism versus particularism in the history of biblical
religion. If, as the ethical-liberal position (found among
both Protestants and Jews) would have it, what really
matters to God is justice and not ceremony, and if this was
an insight that emerged in the prophetic movement, then
the outcome of Hebrew religion is a kind of moral universalism. Israel, by showing the path to righteousness, can be
"a light to the nations." What is important about Israel is
not how Israel was different from any other people but how
Israel provided an insight which is valid for all people.

In contrast, there is the particularist interpretation. Here,
too, social justice is important, but its importance is measured much more within the community. It is included with
other concerns, especially ritual and traditional ones. Looking at the Isaiah passage in question, if ritual as such is not
repudiated, if God's commandments are both ritual *and*
ethical, then it is not necessary to treat ethics as an innova-
tion of the prophets. Morality is just as early in Israel's
national experience as Sabbath observance. Did not Moses,
after all, communicate a significant ethical demand from
God in the Ten Commandments—the charter of Israel's
religion? Israel's obligations are Israel's because God has

communicated them by revelation to Israel, not necessarily
to the rest of humanity.

This special relationship is expressed in the notion of
"covenant." The first expression of covenant, as the narrative stands, is the covenant God offers to Noah, and by
implication to all of humanity, in Genesis 9. God will
preserve humanity and not again virtually annihilate the
species with an all-submerging flood. We find later specific
expressions of covenant with the leaders and people of
Israel. It is a debatable point whether one can argue from
the ordering of the covenant with Noah in the narrative to
the logical priority of God's concern for all people. But
surely one interpretation of the covenant with Abraham in
Genesis 12 is that, in the light of the covenant with Noah, it
implies the special responsibility of the people of Israel to
convey God's blessing to everyone.

For Christians today, it is important to apply this point a
bit further. Because of the universalist thrust of Christian
teaching, it can be disquieting to us today to think that
God's commandments are not acknowledged by all, let
alone heard by all, let alone applicable to all. But particularism is not the same sort of problem for the Jewish tradition.
In some biblical passages, Jewish writers envisioned the
glory of God as vindicated in an ideal future age when Zion,
the hill of Jerusalem, would be raised and all other moun-
tains leveled, when the wealth and tribute of all nations
would flow into Jerusalem. The other nations of the earth,
or "Gentiles," were expected to respect and fear Israel, not
to become Jewish. The classical view of the Hebrew
Scriptures sees the distinction between Israel and the
nations as a lasting one, indeed as one by means of which
God can make his plan and his power manifest. The
existence of other nations (and of other faiths) was never a
theological problem for Hebrew religion or for classical
Judaism. The problem was the prevalence or prosperity of
these nations as compared to the people of Israel.

Judaism in Greek and Roman Times

The Hellenistic age in the Near East began with its conquest by Alexander the Great in 333–323 B.C. Alexander's victory markedly accelerated the pace of cultural interaction. People moved from one region to another and increasingly recognized the similarities of many common human experiences. It became commonplace for Greeks to identify the functions of various Semitic deities as equivalent to those of the gods of Olympus: Baal was the equivalent of Zeus as storm god, Astarte corresponded to Aphrodite (who was known in Rome as Venus), Adonis to Apollo, and so on.

In many ways the Hellenistic age was like our own. It was a time of the growth of cities, the rise of empires, and the migration and mixture of populations. Analogies are treacherous, but it is thought-provoking to compare the role of the Greeks and then the Romans in antiquity with that of the British and then the Americans in modern times.

In the modern world, European culture has left a profound imprint on the rest of the world, shaping the world's technology and its values. This process, known as modernization or westernization, has produced crises for the traditional values of other cultures. A similar thing happened in the case of Hellenistic culture, as it made a political, commercial, and intellectual impact on local communities which came under Greek rule. In its detail it may not have produced results like the Iranian revolution of 1979, with electronic communications used to broadcast the anti-Western ideas of orthodox clergy; but there are parallels in the modern era.

For the Jews of the Greek and Roman era there were several alternatives as to what to do about alien rule, and these alternatives defined various parties within the Jewish community of the day. One option was to treat the Temple worship—its ritual and sacrifices—as the essential thing about Judaism and to collaborate with the Roman rulers in civic matters. This was the position of the Sadducees, and it remained an option as long as the Temple stood, until A.D. 70.

A second option saw the essence of Judaism as the observances one could carry out within the four walls of one's own home, whatever alien ideologies or practices might exist outside, in the forum and the marketplace. This position, making the practice of Judaism a very personal and family affair, was the emphasis of the Pharisees, and it survived the destruction of the Temple and public institutions. In fact, it became the mainstream of rabbinic Judaism and has characterized the practice of Judaism wherever it has been a minority community until our own times.

A third option in a sense held out for the observance of Jewish tradition in the total life of a community; if this could not be carried out in a city under Greek or Roman rule, then a community would have to be established in isolation elsewhere. Such was the character of the monastic settlement built by the Essene sect near the shores of the Dead Sea. The Essenes were scarcely known until the discovery of their library, the Dead Sea Scrolls, in 1947.

A fourth option, and a very political one, was the path of guerrilla resistance aimed at ousting the Romans from Palestine. Rebellion had worked in the Maccabean era two centuries earlier; why not try again? The guerrilla party (the Zealots) apparently scored enough successes to irritate and ultimately infuriate the Romans, but they had taken on too mighty an adversary. When the Romans, who had little taste for insubordination, put their attention to it, they utterly crushed the Zealot movement. Jerusalem was besieged, the Temple and Qumran were destroyed, and practically the only live option remaining for a Jew living in the Hellenistic world was the Pharisaic option.

Well, *almost* the only option. For there was one more, and this was not so much a Palestinian communal option as one that had been forged over time in the Diaspora, that is, the dispersal of Jews outside Palestine. One of the Jewish intellectual centers of the Hellenistic world was Alexandria in Egypt. Alexandria was a meeting place of various cultures, where Greek was the vernacular tongue. Jews living there spoke the Greek language, studied Greek philosophy, and sought to express the essence of their heritage in Greek vocabulary and concepts. The thought of the Alexandrian Jewish writer Philo may be taken as typical of this option. For Philo, what is true in the Jewish heritage is largely that which is compatible with, and confirmed by, reason as the Greek philosophers knew it. God's revelation is essentially ethical, rational, and general, rather than capricious and particularistic.

In the long run the Alexandrian option did not prove to be viable for Hellenistic Judaism, for it did not maintain an identifiable community of Jewish people. Assimilation in the Hellenistic age took its toll, and assimilation remains a challenge for Jews in the twentieth century.

THE NEW TESTAMENT

It is against the background of this rich and diverse array of social and intellectual possibilities confronting first-century Judaism that one must see the growth of the Christian movement, which of course started as a Jewish sect. Against this challenge of identity and quest for authority, the figure of Jesus emerges. What Jesus did and said has been applied to new contexts in each succeeding age, but it is instructive to appreciate the force of Jesus' teachings in the context of his own day.

First of all, the Gospels portray Jesus emphasizing individual piety and practice. This puts him pretty squarely in the category of the Pharisees. Many Christians today may be surprised at this, for the New Testament's mention of Pharisees conjures up a picture of nit-picking legalism mixed with downright hypocrisy. This image exists not because of the contrast between the Christian movement

and the Pharisees, but precisely because of the closeness of
the Christian interpretation to Pharisaism. It was with the
Pharisees more than with others that the early Christians
had their most subtle and detailed arguments, for they
agreed on many of the major points. It was not in a Qumran
community nor in a Zealot uprising nor in the Temple ritual
that the Jewish followers of Jesus did what mattered to their
faith; it was in their personal activity within and outside the
home. Jesus' discussion, as it is reported to us in the
Gospels, is essentially a discussion of points important to
the Pharisees: what practices does God require of people,
and in what priority?

Christianity also had close links with Alexandrian Jewish
philosophy, typified by the writings of Philo. Greek philosophers used the term *logos*, literally "word," to signify the
creative divine intelligence. This term and its conceptual
framework were picked up by early Christian writers,
including the author of the Fourth Gospel. John's Gospel
begins, "In the beginning was the Word," and continues,
"The true light that illuminates every one came into the
world." Notice the emphasis on "every one." Jewish universalism as well as Jewish particularism was part of the
background of the earliest Christians. Not all the Greek
ideas of the New Testament writers necessarily reached
them through Gentile channels.

For the Christian reader, the early Christian community's
view of the relationship between religions comes as both a
culmination and a starting point: a culmination of the
Israelite and Jewish background which we have been
sketching, and the start of the two-thousand-year experience of the church. It may therefore come as something of a
disappointment that the New Testament does not register a
clean break with previous views. This is because the
church began as a Jewish sect and shared many of the
Jewish understandings of the purposes of God for the
world.

For example, the earliest Christians used a Jewish frame
of reference to conceive the power and scope of God's
concern. God was lord of the whole creation, as Second
Isaiah and then the Pharisees understood him to be, but
God still had a special concern for the Jews. Gentiles were
not a problem in Jewish thought or the earliest Christian
thought. It was not the fact of the alien identity or belief of
Gentiles, but the fact of their current power (particularly
the Romans) which was the problem for the faithful. For
hundreds of years the message of consolation to a politically
threatened Israel had been to take heart and maintain faith,
for ultimately the Lord would vindicate his name and the
fortunes of his people. The longer the vindication was put
off, the more glorious it would be when it came; from the
literal and verbal terms of prophetic eschatology Jewish
writers had extrapolated what we call apocalyptic literature. In apocalyptic writings, there is a symbolic and
visionary description of the end of things. The final separation of good and evil men, Jews and Gentiles, is envisioned
as taking place amid trumpet blasts, worldwide battles,
sometimes a reshaping of the landscape, and a restoration of
the anointed Davidic kingship. The early Christians apparently thought that such an end of things was imminent.

With other Jews, the Christians shared the expectation of
an anointed one, a Messiah. It was not the Messianic
expectation which was distinctive; it was the claim of the
content and fulfillment of that expectation. Christians believed that although popular sentiment might have fallen
off drastically following Jesus' triumphal entry into Jerusalem, he had in fact been the anointed one, and the long-
awaited kingdom had in fact been inaugurated. This had
happened despite Jesus' humiliating execution on the
cross, because earthly success was not the criterion of *this*
Messiahship ("My kingship is not of this world," they
quoted him). Anyway, Jesus would be coming back soon to
complete the vindication of his message as embodying
God's plan and promise. Most of the New Testament

authors expected that return immediately, and only as time
passed and the return did not occur was the *parousia,* or
"second coming," put off to a more distant end of the age.

Some scholars hold that the apolitical nature of Jesus'
messianic rule, together with the inclusion of Gentiles
along with Jews as the community who would inherit the
promise, constitutes a universalistic option. It was not the
only one present to the first generation of Christians after
Jesus' death, but it proved to be the most attractive choice.
There were also military-political options. One of the
disciples was a Zealot; and when Jesus was taken prisoner
in Gethsemane, at least some of the disciples were armed.

The Jewish character of the early church is seen more
clearly in the debate over whether one needed to be a Jew
first in order to become a Christian. The Jerusalem Christians believed that circumcision, Sabbath observance, and
dietary taboos were mandatory for Christians. A contrasting
view, that the old law had been transcended by divine love
and human faith, was set forth particularly in overseas
communities by Paul, who may have done as much as any
one person to shape early Christianity in the form in which
we know it. Paul traveled back to Jerusalem, where in the
year 49 it was agreed that circumcision was not necessary.
The church was thus set on a path on which increasingly it
became an independent new religion rather than remaining
a Jewish sect. As an inclusive and missionary religion, it
claimed universality for its message and proposed salvation
for all. The church's theological problem would thus become and remain what we face today: what about those who
do not become Christian? How much of what is good or true
which they possess as a heritage from other sources conflicts with the uniqueness of Christianity, and how much of
their future goodness or truth contradicts the finality of
Christianity? These questions were already implicit in the
dynamics of the first-generation church as it embarked on
its mission.

The most disruptive event in first-century Palestine was the catastrophic rebellion of the Jews against Rome in 66–70. On the surface, the New Testament is strangely silent about this war and its effect. One would expect it to be discussed, or referred to, in the narrative of the apostolic church in Acts. One might expect some of the New Testament letters to refer to it. One encounters what can even seem a conspiracy of silence.

Yet at another level, it is clear that the New Testament authors are doing all they can to dissociate their movement from military ambitions and from Jewish political nationalism. They stress the pacifism and the universality of Jesus' teaching. One of the more explicit references to the siege of Jerusalem is in Luke 19. Jesus, approaching the city via the Mount of Olives, wishes it knew the things that make for peace and weeps as he envisions its destruction. Luke must have written the passage in the light of the actual experience of the war of 66–70; but even taken as Jesus' anticipation of the events, the pacifism is clear. Thus, however much or little the church was leaning toward a universalistic approach to Gentiles prior to 66–70, the disastrous consequences of Jewish nationalism in those years encouraged the church to transcend its Judaic base and state its message in universal terms.

JESUS

In examining the figure of Jesus for direction as to how to view other religions, we find a variety of forms of guidance. The tension between different statements and interpretations will, in the long run, require us to choose and take a stand.

At one end of the range are the passages which assume that Jews are better than Gentiles. In the Sermon on the Mount (Matthew 6), Jesus counsels his disciples not to be anxious about having enough to eat or to wear, "for after all these things do the Gentiles seek." As the Christian church lays claim to the promises and privileges (as well as the responsibilities of faithfulness) that were Israel's, presumably it has the warrant to put Christians ahead of non-Christians. Any first-century Jew, including Jesus, might endorse the preference of his own community to others. It is possible to read Jesus, through some texts such as these, as perpetuating a notion of superiority over others.

Another position that some have tried to derive from the figure of Jesus is the confident insistence that in him, and only in him, is truth or salvation to be found. The oft-quoted passage John 3:16 says: "God so loved the world that he gave his only-begotten son, that whosoever believeth on him should not perish but have everlasting life." This, you might argue, is a theological statement *about* Jesus, but in John's Gospel, Jesus also makes similar statements in the first person, such as the crucial passage (John 14:6), "I am the way, and the truth, and the life, no one comes to the Father, but by me." Two millennia of Christian evangelists have shared the confidence of their first-century predecessors that on Jesus' own authority they had the truth, the whole truth, and nobody but them had the truth.

If the foregoing were all that there were to Jesus' word and example, the central problem of this book might be easily dismissed. But the figure of Jesus also sets aside communal boundaries and exclusive notions of truth. For example, the parables of Jesus appeal not to particular scriptural revelations but to universal human experiences. Certain parables state a universalist ideal quite explicitly: the parable of the good Samaritan, for example, which tells us that the truly good person was not the priest of one's own community but the magnanimous outsider.

Indeed, the most telling argument and the most profound challenge to take other people and their traditions seriously comes from Jesus' own word and example. He was the one who defied social pressure to associate with the "tax collectors and sinners." He was the one for whom wealth and

status meant nothing in themselves, for whom a poor
person's simple devotion could outweigh the pious prayers
of even the high priests. When Jesus met the woman at the
well in Shechem, he showed himself ready to accept
another human being as a child of God regardless of
national identity or personal background. Jesus' attitude
toward other persons as individuals exhibits a consistency
with his golden rule, to treat the other person the way you
would wish to be treated yourself.

Jesus voices his desire that his way of discipleship be for
everyone. "Go therefore," some manuscripts of Matthew's
Gospel quote him, "and make disciples of all nations"
(28:19). This passage, though frequently cited in support of
a universal Christian claim to truth, also serves as evidence
for a central Christian concern for all humanity. It is this
urge toward universality which was later to turn up in the
adjective "catholic" applied to the church, meaning "universal." We cannot be sure that Jesus foresaw the divisions
which would emerge in later centuries among the body of
his followers; perceptive observer of human nature that he
was, he well might have predicted them. But it is significant, and central to any present-day effort to state a Christian understanding of the religions, to note that for every
branch of Christendom—Eastern Orthodox, Roman Catholic, Protestant—the figure of Jesus remains central. His
word, his example, and his person are the norm by which
all Christian thought and behavior must be judged.

The tension between particularist doctrinal claims and
universalist moral imperatives does not end here. Some see
divine revelation in particulars and human reason in uni-
versals; they contend that Christianity as a revealed religion is true especially in respect of its particular benefits for
Christians and not in any openness to others. But it is
arbitrary to exclude Jesus' moral universalism from the
category "revelation," for quite apart from its human universality it is presented to us in the New Testament as
God's intention for all people. Jesus declared his message

to his Palestinian Jewish contemporaries, and they proceeded to tell the world what they had heard. The image of Jesus who is open to others is just as important as the other image of Jesus who stands in judgment of others. Perhaps the church has lost sight of this first image through the centuries, and the recovery of this vision would be a step forward in resolving the tension that many Christians now find between Christian commitment and religious pluralism.

2
THE CHURCH'S CLASSIC POSITION

Throughout the centuries the church has encountered different cultures, philosophies, and religions. When Christians have found themselves in a non-Christian environment, they have taken into account the moral and intellectual accomplishments of others. Even when Christian thought and institutions have come closer to dominating a culture, such as in medieval Europe, Christians have still been aware that in other times and places not everybody called on the name of Jesus.

Typical discussions of this topic have classified Christian views systematically, sorting Christian writers into a range of four or five positions regarding the value of other religions. Philosophical theologians find this approach congenial; among recent efforts, good examples are the typologies by Owen Thomas in *Attitudes Toward Other Religions* (1969, pp. 19–28), and by Charles Davis in *Christ and the World Religions* (1970, pp. 49–59).

In this chapter I propose something different. As a historian, I am convinced that specific circumstances are as important as overall patterns. Generalizing too soon about Christian attitudes to other religions masks the particular development of attitudes to particular religions. My scheme does imply a classification, but it is one that is centuries old: the classification of religions themselves. These are the

34

religions from which the concept "religion," as we know it, emerged as a generalization and an abstraction.

RELIGION

The very phrase "other religions" implies part of our problem. On the one hand, the word "other" indicates some difference, presumably some essential difference, between our community and the rest of the world. But the second half of the phrase, the term "religion," implies some recognizable continuities, some shared features, by which our heritage and the heritages of other people are all called "religions." To refer to Judaism or Islam as "other religions" is to imply that Christianity is also a "religion." There must be at least certain essential features for anything to be a "religion"—essential features which Christianity shares not only with Judaism and Islam but with all the greater and lesser religious traditions of the world. Some twentieth-century Protestant theologians, such as Karl Barth, argue for the uniqueness of Christianity by distinguishing between God's gift as revelation and human strivings as religion; but such a distinction flies in the face of the commonsense realization that at least in its human manifestations Christianity is a religion with a great deal in common with others.

What does it mean to be "a religion"? This is not an easy question to answer. The word "religion" underwent a significant shift in meaning around the seventeenth century. If one looks at the medieval senses of the Latin word *religio*, from which "religion" comes, it will be seen to have connoted something like piety or religiosity. "True religion" was true fidelity to, and true service of, God. It did not mean, in this earlier usage, a true system of belief (ours) as opposed to a false one (theirs). As Wilfred Smith has observed, Calvin's title familiarly translated *Institutes of the Christian Religion* might much better be rendered

Grounding in Christian Piety. The word "religion" came to
be used in the plural only around the sixteenth century,
when "a religion" came to mean any one of "the religions,"
the systems of thought and discipline to which one might
adhere by accident of birth or even make a conscious
decision to espouse. "Other religions" as a phrase, then,
has only been available since the sixteenth century.

The question itself was not new in the sixteenth century,
not even in the Middle Ages, because the concept behind
the term "religions" is much older than the term itself. In
biblical times the Hebrews were aware that other peoples
worshiped other gods, and the earliest Christians were
aware that other peoples followed other teachings. Although the word "religions" does not appear in the plural
in the Greek and Latin church fathers, words meaning
"opinions" and "teachings" frequently do. To review the
church's traditional position is to examine what Christian
thinkers and church councils have said about the opinions,
teachings, and doctrines of others.

To understand religion in terms of doctrine is a classic
Christian tendency, but doctrine is by no means the only
central feature of religion. Religion entails action as well as
thought, action both in a ritual and in a moral sense. We
may try to analyze others by asking what they believe, but
an equally important question is what they do. In fact, the
record of Europe's discovery of Asian, African, and Native
American cultures shows that the ceremonies and customs—the observable outward behavior—of various peoples were extensively described before their belief systems
were understood in any detail.

The Christian tendency to define religion in terms of
doctrine is not uniquely Christian. There are other religions, such as Islam, which also require a specific profession of faith in creedal terms. But many traditions, particularly religions of a particular national or cultural group such
as Hinduism, Judaism, or Shinto, do not. In teaching
university courses in the comparative study of religion I

have frequently asked students at the start of term to state their understanding of "religion" in a sentence or a paragraph, and at least half the responses have centered around individual belief in God. The agenda of catechetical instruction has had its effects on those students who profess a belief, and on those who do not.

The other essential dimension of religion is the corporate. What distinguishes a religion from a philosophy is that it is shared, perpetuated, and ritually celebrated in a community. Without community, it is hard to have tradition; and without tradition, it is hard to have what we are accustomed to call religion.

A strict definition of "religion" is not easy, for there are about as many definitions as there are scholars in the field. What we commonly call "religions" have few, if any, universally shared specific characteristics. Not belief in God, for there are forms of early Buddhism which lack this. Not mythology, for there is hardly any narrative myth in Islam. Not even ritual, unless perhaps the very holding of a silent Quaker meeting is itself a ritual act. And yet, some sense of power beyond humankind, expressed symbolically as well as literally, emotionally as well as rationally, actively as well as speculatively, corporately as well as individually, may well characterize the traditions we wish to include without also gathering in such present-day commitments as Marxism or secular humanist philosophy.

The plain fact is that our concept "religion" starts with the example of the tradition we know, and describes others in terms of it. There are traditions which we call religions that have no equivalent word for "religion" in their classical languages—Chinese, for example. Why do we call Confucius (an agnostic when it came to the gods) a religious teacher and Socrates a secular one? Presumably because the tradition of thought and action identified in China with Confucius was extended to cover the characteristic concerns we associate with religion, while the figure of Socrates in retrospect stands outside the Western traditions we call religions, however much they have historically absorbed his thought. We may identify a question of meaning or value as a religious question no matter who asks it. To identify an answer to it as part of a religion is to associate the topic with a historically developed, and developing, tradition.

THE RELIGIONS

In the generation since the end of World War II the comparative study of the "great" or "world" religions has increased in extent and sophistication. We now have a bewildering array of textbooks and specialized studies on the major religious traditions, and there has been a general consensus as to what those traditions are.

There are three great religions which have spread by missionary activity. Their communities transcend the boundaries of any one population, and their literatures have flourished in more than one language. These, in alphabetical and historical order, are Buddhism, Christianity, and Islam.

To these one must add the national pre-Buddhist, pre-Christian, and pre-Muslim heritage of India, which since about 1800 has been labeled Hinduism. Its adherents number in the hundreds of millions, like those of our first three. Another national religion, Judaism, has been a "must" for any short list of religions, even though there are from fifty to a hundred times as many Buddhists, or Christians, or Muslims in the world as there are Jews. This inclusion is partly because of Judaism's significant historical relationship to Christianity and partly because of Jews' status as a minority in Western society.

After these first five religions, consensus fades. In Britain, standard textbooks also list the five-century-old Sikh tradition, because of the modern migration of many Sikhs from India to England. In America, the usual candidates for expansion of the list beyond five are China's great traditions other than Buddhism—the Confucian and the Taoist. Both are historically and philosophically significant, though their active practice as living religions since the victory of Mao in 1949 has been visible chiefly among Chinese outside the People's Republic of China.

The remaining candidates are Shinto, the indigenous non-Buddhist heritage of Japan; Jainism, an Indian tradition about as old as Buddhism; and Zoroastrianism, the historically significant national religion of Iran before Islam, whose community has dwindled to a hundred thousand adherents mainly in India and Iran. Whether five great religions, or six, or ten, or eleven, the roster of the world's living religions is a modern idea; it has emerged only since the middle of the nineteenth century. The earliest Western author to list a half dozen religions according to the above criteria was apparently the British theologian F. D. Maurice, writing in 1846.

Prior to the mid-nineteenth century, what was Christendom's notion of "the religions"? Interestingly, for a number of centuries from the Middle Ages till modern times there does appear to have been a consensus. When Europe began to take Islam seriously during the Crusades, the fourfold categorization of Christians, Jews, Muslims, and pagans caught on. As the word "religion" came to be used in the plural, encyclopedic handbooks listing the religious ceremonies and customs of the known world regularly used these four headings. The sequence varied from author to author, but the headings were the same. For early modern Europe, the Jews constituted an alien community within Christendom, the Muslims were the alien community outside, and "paganism" represented an alien world from the past.

JUDAISM

Since the early church, Christian authors have character-
istically given a special place to Judaism. The Christian
tradition is self-conscious about its historical and theological roots in ancient Judaism, and the phrase "Judeo-Chris-
tian tradition" has been used in the twentieth century to
describe historical continuity and stress shared ideals and
values. But the Christian church is ambivalent toward
Judaism, stressing its common roots and yet affirming its
own distinctiveness.

In the twenty centuries of Christian debate with Judaism,
one major theme is "chosenness." The two religions agree
that ancient Israel was chosen by God for both special
privileges and special obligations. God made specific
promises to Israel. The question is, and has been for
centuries: Who now is Israel? Who is heir to the promise?
The church's claim has been that the Christian community,
from the very moment of Jesus' ministry, has taken over the
identity of the covenant community. The church claims to
be the new Israel, theologically completely replacing the
old. God chose Israel to be his people, the church claims,
and in a subsequent covenant or dispensation God chose
the church.

There is a degree of ambivalence in the Christian sense
of chosenness. Christian theologians have sought the benefits of being specially chosen or elected by God, and at the
same time they have also sought the benefits of a universal
openness. In the Bible, God's covenant relationship was
made with all humanity through Noah, but then focused on
the Hebrew people through Abraham and his descendants.
It is to the covenant of Abraham that the church regards
itself as heir, but that covenant is also seen in the New
Testament and in Christian theology as having been transcended by a message for all people. No longer is it only
Jews, but also Gentiles, who may share in God's promise.

The church claims, in effect, to cash in on all the benefits promised specifically to the heirs of Abraham on behalf of an inclusive community equivalent to the heirs of Noah. To use a metaphor from card games, Judaism is seen as a hand that has been trumped.

One theological consequence of the Christian claim to possess the entirety of the covenant promise is that nothing in the Jewish tradition after New Testament times is seen as significant. Until our own century there has been an almost total neglect of the ongoing development of Jewish faith. Judaism has been treated, even in our own time, as a religion which stagnated once it had produced Christianity. Post-biblical Judaism is seen as the empty cocoon left behind by the butterfly of the New Israel, the church. This attitude extends even to older textbooks: Robert E. Hume's 1924 text on the world's living religions, a standard book in the United States for two decades, treated Judaism as a preparation for the gospel whose story was complete with the coming of Christ. (In a revision issued after World War II the publishers saw fit to add to that chapter.)

The second theme is the opposition of law and gospel. We owe to the apostle Paul the Christian position that while claiming the old promises to biblical Israel the church is exempted from many of the old biblical obligations. Paul was an observant Jew and had been strict in following the prescriptions of Jewish law. Following his conversion to Christianity, he proclaimed that the law had been set aside by Jesus' message and self-sacrifice. The old religion, for Paul, amounted to bondage to the law; the new religion promised liberation from the law. Formerly people were justified by their righteous or observant acts. For Paul, people are justified by their faith, which is a free gift from God.

Paul's polarity between law and gospel has stayed with Christian thinking for nearly twenty centuries. But early in the church's experience, it became clear that to push the contrast would separate the church as the New Israel too far from the old Israel and weaken its claim to be heir of the covenant promise. The second-century A.D. Christian thinker Marcion, influenced by the dualistic teachings of Gnosticism, sought to stress the contrast between a god of wrath in the Old Testament and a god of love in the New, and to limit the authoritative writings for Christians to the gospels and the letters of Paul. The historic consequence of Marcion's emphasis was a reaction which affirmed the Old Testament as Scripture and affirmed Christianity's roots in the faith and the expectations of ancient Israel.

The third theme is the basis of moral obligation. Christians have not always treated the idea of law or commandment as something replaced by the gospel. The Ten Commandments are part of Christian piety, frequently committed to memory and sometimes repeated in services of worship. Jesus, when challenged to name the greatest commandment, did not pick one of the ten, but went instead to Deuteronomy 6 and Leviticus 19: "Love the Lord your God ... and love your neighbor as yourself." "On these two commandments," he went on to say, "depend all the Law and the Prophets," that is, they sum up the scriptural collections known in his day as the Law and the Prophets, the entirety of what then had status as Scripture.

It was not law as such, but the question of which commandment took priority that was the bone of contention between the Jewish authorities of Jesus' day and this new Jewish sect, the Christians. What was the standard by which one commandment should be followed rather than another, if they conflicted in practice? During twenty centuries Christians have characterized the traditional Jewish law as inflexible and hairsplitting. There is substantial support for this view in the Gospels' presentation of Jesus as putting human good ahead of legal observance: "The sabbath was made for man, not man for the sabbath." Jesus, moreover, decries the hypocrisy of the scribes and Pharisees, to whom outward observance of the letter of the law is apparently prior to a loving heart.

Jesus takes into his own hand the question of authority of interpretation. A recurring formula in the Gospels is "You have heard ... but I say to you. ..." In some cases the appeal is to one scriptural authority rather than another, but in others his appeal is to general common sense or personal authority. To argue with tradition is not new with Jesus; the prophet Jeremiah proclaimed a new covenant in people's hearts to update the covenant of Sinai, and both Jeremiah and Ezekiel refute the traditional notion of inherited guilt, citing and denying the proverb, "The fathers have eaten sour grapes, and the children's teeth are set on edge." But for Christians it is with Jesus most of all that a self-confidence in the face of traditional authority serves as evidence of a special status. The people were astonished because "he taught them as one who had authority, and not as the scribes."

The tradition of the Pharisees survived the Jewish war against Rome in the first century to become the basis of rabbinic legal interpretation in the Talmud in the second through the sixth century. The characterization of Pharisaism as legalistic is accurate, in the sense that it did indeed devote much attention to the conditions under which specific commandments should be followed. But this hardly does justice to the humane concern implicit in such Talmudic distinctions as the following: if one is rescuing someone from a burning building and has no time to clear the house of leaven before the Passover celebration, he may annul the leaven "in his heart," but if he is simply out for a stroll, he must return and carry out the ritual obligation of clearing the house. Such attempts by the Pharisees to render the law livable are not taken into account in Christian representations of Pharisaism.

The fourth important point deals with the messiahship of Jesus. Christians saw in Jesus the expected restoration of the Davidic royal line. This view is central to a Christian understanding of God's will. For a Jew, the central point is not the identity of the Messiah but the identity of the

people of God's covenant. For years Christians have defined Jews as people who do not believe in Jesus, rather
than representing what Jews care most about. It is as silly to
characterize Jews as those who refute the messiahship of
Jesus as to characterize Christians as those who deny the
prophethood of Muhammad.

Traditional Christian views of Judaism do not stop at the
simple statement that Jews do not believe in Jesus as
Messiah. They blame Jews for having stubbornly *refused* to
believe in him. Theologically, the Jews are not simply
people who don't "happen" to be Christian. They are
people to whom the gospel was preached and who through
stupidity or perversity have refused to respond.

Nor do long-standing Christian attitudes stop there. An
all-too-common view, historically taken by Christians as
grounds for persecuting Jewish minorities, is that the Jews
actually killed Jesus. Clearly, in the Gospel accounts, it was
at the instigation of the Jewish authorities that Jesus was
arrested and brought before the Roman regime for trial.
And it was at the bidding of the crowd of Jews to whom
Pilate turned that the criminal Barabbas was released rather
than Jesus. John's Gospel in particular frequently uses the
blanket phrase "the Jews" for those who sought and effect-
ed Jesus' execution, and Matthew explicitly quotes them,
"His blood be on us, and on our descendants."

Must the Gospels be read as a warrant for the suffering
and persecution which have been visited on the Jews
through the centuries? Hardly. For one thing, the notion of
inherited guilt is open to challenge on scriptural grounds in
Jeremiah and Ezekiel. More important, many Christians
have exempted the Jews as a people from the charge of
killing Christ. Some have done so by narrowing the blame:
it was only a few Jewish leaders, after all, not the whole
people, who schemed against Jesus. Other Christians have
widened the blame instead: it was not the Jews as such, but
human wickedness and sinfulness generally which brought
Jesus to the cross. "The Jews" symbolize everyone. In this

view we have all, through our sinfulness, put Christ to
death. Christ is the redemptive answer to the sin of Adam,
that is, of humanity.

In the twentieth century, two events have so dramatically
affected the topic of Christian attitudes to Judaism that they
now must be added to the list as a fifth heading in
themselves: the European holocaust and the establishment
of the modern state of Israel. The cold-blooded murder of
approximately six million Jews—one third of the Jewish
population of the world—by the Nazis during World War II
may have been abetted by some of the theological views
expressed above, but since then the holocaust itself has
produced a new sense of guilt. "We Christians," it is held,
permitted the climate of thought that allowed the Nazi
pogrom, or at least we didn't do all we should have toward
preventing it.

This attitude has also called for compensation to the
Jewish people. We owe it now to make amends, whether by
purging our own tradition of its anti-Jewish statements and
its "triumphalist" claims to fulfill and supersede ancient
Israel, or by supporting Jews against Arabs in the continuing struggle for possession of the land formerly called
Palestine. Indeed, it is doubtful that Israel's cause in the
Middle East since World War II would have had as much
Western support if it were not for Christian shock and guilt
over what befell the Jews in Europe during that war. Many
Christians have been willing to excuse policies pursued by
the State of Israel which they would have flatly condemned
had any other state attempted them.

For some Christians who take a strict literal view of the
Bible, the establishment of the State of Israel is foretold in
Scripture, and Old Testament promises to ancient Israel,
such as possession of land, are still binding. For a few, the
expected end of the age is associated with various signs of
renewal, such as the restoration of Israel's power and the
conversion of the Jews. They see the modern state as the
first of these, and eagerly await the second. Needless to say,

Jews are astute enough to distinguish between such political support and the theological imperialism which motivates it.

But the notion that the Jewish people have a right to their
traditional identity, as an enduring witness to God's covenants, and are no longer proper targets for conversion to
Christianity, has gained support in far wider circles. This
recognition, along with present-day dialogue efforts, illus-
trates the fact that Christian attitudes toward the Jews are
undergoing significant change in our own times.

ISLAM

When we turn to Christianity's other long-term rival,
Islam, we find that the terms of the rivalry are different. It is
not covenant and law which have classically been at stake,
but prophethood and politics. Through the centuries the
Muslim nations have posed concrete military challenges to
the West, and Islamic religion has posed intellectual challenges so forcefully that there have been almost no conver-
sions from Islam to Christianity. Islamic doctrine has explicitly denied certain Christian teachings, and the Islamic
community has set the severest penalty—death—for aposta-
sy from Islam. From the Christian side, so much animosity
since the days of the Crusades has carried over to the
present that Islam remains the most hated and feared of the
world religions, in the general view of the West. With the
notable exception of the Black Muslims, Islam is the least
likely choice of those individuals who seek an alternative to
Christianity. But even in American black communities,
Islam has its own shock value.

In one major respect Christianity's theological relationship to Islam is the opposite of its relationship to Judaism.
Whereas Christian theology has taken pride in supplanting
ancient Judaism, Christians have viewed with alarm the
prospect of being supplanted by Islam. Judaism is Chris-

tianity's predecessor; Islam is Christianity's successor.
Muslims and Christians agree that there is one God. But
they disagree that Muhammad brought the culmination of
God's message.

Islamic teaching has had the status of a heresy in the
minds of many Christians, for it explicitly denies doctrines
which Christians hold. These include the incarnation of
God in Jesus. In the Qur'an we read, "He is God the one,
God the pure; he did not beget and was not begotten, and
there is none like unto him." To Muslims the Christian
doctrines of the incarnation and the Trinity smack of
polytheism, or belief in several gods. Islamic doctrine also
denies the passion and resurrection of Jesus, holding that
he did not die on the cross and that the event was only an
apparition. Jesus does, however, command respect among
Muslims as one of the prophets before Muhammad; and the
Qur'an does, interestingly enough, affirm his virgin birth.
The Christian minorities in Islamic countries have had
formal tolerated status because Christianity is a scriptural
religion admired by the Qur'an; Christians are "people of
the book," as distinct from the pagan polytheists of ancient
Arabia for whom the Qur'an has no patience.

Much of Christendom's classic image of Islam has centered on the figure of Muhammad. For centuries the West
termed the religion "Mohammedanism," and is only now
abandoning the name. It is offensive to Muslims when seen
alongside the name "Christianity," both because of the
implied veneration of the Prophet as divine and because of
the implied initiative on his part. Islam, in the view of many
Christians, was Muhammad's own creation, even a fraudulent concoction. Islam teaches just the opposite: the Qur'an,
for Muslims, is God's revelation, word for word, its content
in no way attributable to Muhammad's political astuteness,
literary skill, or religious insight. One classic Christian
stereotype of Muhammad sees him as an impostor, who for
selfish reasons posed as a prophet and deceived the world.

Through the centuries Christians have indulged in attacks on Muhammad's character. He has been portrayed as an epileptic, a Casanova, a tyrant, and, in our own times, a male chauvinist.

Western attitudes toward Islam have varied over the years. Conflicting stereotypes have sometimes been held simultaneously. The Islamic peoples have been seen, for example, as fierce and at the same time hospitable; scheming and at the same time impulsive. It is of course characteristic of stereotypes to be illogical.

Western perceptions of Islam can be divided into three periods, the first from the Arab conquests to about the seventeenth century, the second from the seventeenth century to the end of World War II, and the third from 1945 to the present.

Fear characterizes the first of these periods. Following the unification of Arabia by Muhammad's followers, Arab armies conquered the southern and eastern shores of the Mediterranean, and east into Iran and central Asia, within a century. From Spain to Iraq, Arabic replaced Latin, Greek, and other tongues as the vernacular language, as Christian populations largely became Muslim. Sometimes tangible benefits such as tax advantages or political opportunity were an inducement to becoming Muslim; in the eyes of the Christian West, however, Islam spread chiefly by the power of the sword. The Islamic notion of *jihad,* struggle in defense of the faith, was seen as an offensive holy war. As with many wars since, each side saw its own cause as defensive. The reason given for mounting the Crusades was to recover control of the shrines in the Holy Land from the "infidel" Muslims, and sinister stereotypes were circulated in Europe to justify these campaigns.

As Arab military successes were followed by Turkish victories, the Turks replaced the Arabs as the object of Europe's fear and hatred; but the image of Muslims as warriors and of Islam as a militaristic religion remained. Martin Luther, in the sixteenth century, interpreted the

Turkish siege of Vienna as God's judgment on Christendom for what he saw as the sins of the papacy in Rome. This is a religious reading of current events paralleling the Hebrew prophets' views of the Assyrians two thousand years earlier. Until modern times, the image of the "terrible Turk" was standard in Europe in matters large and small; the vigorous, martial music of Brahms is nicknamed Hungarian, but that of Mozart and Beethoven is called Turkish.

The second period covers the European colonial domination of Asia and Africa. The historical circumstances emerged gradually. People who were alive in 1453 when Constantinople fell to the Turks were still living when the Portuguese sailed around Africa, opening up a sea route to India; but it would be many years before the consequences of Europe's command of Asian trade routes would be evident. Europe's growing lead in technology as well as military power helped to remove much of the fear regarding Muslims, and to replace it with a patronizing curiosity mingled with disdain.

To the colonial era we owe such images as the indulgent fascination with the Muslim world as a land of mystery and sensuality. How many ornate screens and courtyards of Moorish architecture were, for example, copied in American movie theaters in the 1920s? The veil, the belly dance, the Turkish harem, and the Qur'an's notion of paradise as filled with young maidens, all formed part of a view of Islam as a sensual religion—at least for males. Coupled with this was a fascination with the desert, exemplified in the career of Lawrence of Arabia, a view of the life of the bedouin as romantic, and of traditional Arab hospitality as embodying the Islamic ideal of peace. Elements of this romanticizing of the Islamic world carry over in the appeal of the Nation of Islam, or "Black Muslim" movement, in which Islam is seen as accomplishing in practice a brotherhood and community of mankind which Christianity only preaches in theory.

The third period, the decades since 1945, has seen the return of an attitude of fear and distrust toward Muslims. A number of factors have contributed to this. The West, particularly since 1973, has felt a hemorrhaging of its economy and an erosion of its prodigal life-style, as increased sums flow to certain Islamic countries in payment for the oil they possess. Fear of the power this wealth confers may be overrated, but it is fear nevertheless. Another factor is the Israeli-Arab conflict; the Jewish quest for possession of the Holy Land, in part religiously motivated itself, is seen as facing an Islamic world bent on holy war much like that which the Crusaders faced.

Still another factor is the emergence of Islamic orthodoxy as a political force in the Muslim countries. A desire to structure a state along Islamic principles resulted in the creation of Pakistan when Britain withdrew from India in 1947. And the Islamic religious leadership provided a political base for toppling the Shah of Iran in 1979; religion remains a potent factor even in the most Westernized—secularized—Muslim countries. The current fear of Islam as a political force stems not so much from its military power as such; the West and the Soviet Union retain the lead, and both supply arms to these countries. It comes, rather, from the power of a strict literal interpretation of religious revelation and a code of traditional law. This motivates large numbers of people and gives them a sense of identity and purpose. Islam seems now not idyllic but ideological; the desert seems filled with tanks rather than tents.

Yet certain elements of the West's picture of Islam remain valid, and on these a new understanding can be built. The religion is, after all, a near relative of Christianity, with a similar notion of God as creator, revealer, and comforter. Compared with the wide variety of religions, Christianity's quarrel with Islam is a family quarrel.

PAGANISM

The third and most diverse category of Christianity's traditional rivals is "paganism," which is an interesting term in itself. The Latin original meant "rural"; the word "peasant" has the same origin. The use of this Latin term to mean non-Christian reflects the historical circumstances of the expansion of Christianity in the Roman Empire. Christianity spread particularly in the cities and along the routes of travel and trade, while the older Roman cults survived in the countryside after the cities had been won over. The word "heathen" is the Germanic or Anglo-Saxon counterpart of the Latin "pagan." It, too, refers to the pre-Christian faith of people living in the heath, the remote rural areas.

After 1500 when Europe began to discover the great traditions of India and China (as well as the tribal religions of Africa and the western hemisphere), Christians used the category of "pagan" to describe them. No longer was paganism simply the old polytheism of Greece, Rome, and northern Europe. Now there were contemporary "pagans," many of them urban and sophisticated, to whom the gospel might be preached and whose potential salvation was a matter of concern to Christians.

Religions other than Judaism and Islam present certain comparable and common issues for the Christian theologian. The Christian argument with these other religions is not a historic rivalry based on different interpretations of a shared prophetic heritage, as in the Jewish and Muslim cases. Rather, these religions pose the question whether that heritage is necessary for salvation.

I shall discuss Christian attitudes toward "pagans" under two general heads: first, those which start from a difference between Christianity and other faiths; and second, those which start from similarities.

The biblical injunction, "You shall have no other gods

before me," has been a frequent theme of Christianity's approach to other religions. The early Christians in ancient Rome faced martyrdom rather than bow down to the Roman deities or to the imperial cult. Christian missionaries to tribal peoples have frequently called for a repudiation of the local gods as idols. Even in the contemporary encounter with the great world religions, there are conservative Christians who take a hard line. For example, when an interfaith service welcomed the Tibetan Buddhist leader, the Dalai Lama, to Toronto, Christian pickets carried placards reading, "Buddhism is idolatry," and "Thou shalt have no other gods before Me."

Some modern Christian writers have argued that enlightenment, the goal of certain Asian religions, is different from the Christian goal of salvation. Enlightenment, they argue, is a state. of insight or awareness rather than of divine forgiveness of human sin. Or, they maintain, enlightenment is the result of human striving, not salvation by God. Such a view, of course, hardly makes room for the presence of any initiatives on God's part to help people toward enlightenment; some East Asian Buddhists hold that God does help in this way.

The contrast between divine initiative and human striving is at its strongest in the twentieth-century theology of Karl Barth and his followers. Drawing especially on Paul, Augustine, and Luther, Barth argues that God's revelation through Christ and God's gift of salvation constitute revelation from the top down, as it were, while human strivings from the bottom up constitute religion. From the Barthian perspective, which has influenced such missionary theologians as Hendrik Kraemer, only the Christian revelation comes from God. All other religions come from humanity, and as such stand under the judgment of the gospel. It is amusing to see Barth worry over the possibility that Pure Land Buddhism in Japan might also have proclaimed the notion of salvation by faith. In an elaborate four-page note, Barth salvages uniqueness of content at least, if not uniqueness of manner, for Christian salvation.

One other classic interpretation comes from the second-century Christian writer Justin Martyr. In his first *Apology*, he suggests that the seeming similarities of pagan teachings with Christian ones are imitations of Christianity, placed there by the devil to test the faith of true believers. Justin's view that paganism is the work of demons recognizes substance in the faith of others but denies its value for salvation.

To sum up: This position denies either the existence or the effectiveness of the gods or the faith of others. Christianity is "radically" new and different, and is unique in conveying God's gifts to all people.

Second, the argument for similarity covers a more subtle range of historic Christian positions. Its strongest form is the view that the God who has made himself known to us in Christ has revealed himself *equally* to other peoples under other names. This view is more characteristic of late-nineteenth- and twentieth-century liberal and universalist views than of the mainstream of Christian theology through the centuries. It is, however, increasingly attractive among the general public in a pluralistic age.

The view that God has revealed himself *partially* to other peoples under other names is a much more characteristic position of Christian thinkers toward the "pagan" religions. It is implied in the New Testament in Paul's sermon to the Athenians in Acts 17. Paul tells the Athenians that he appreciates how religious they are. They even have an altar "to an unknown god"; and Paul tells them that this god they already worship is the same God he proclaims.

To Justin Martyr and to Clement of Alexandria in the second century the church owes the concept that the best insights of pagan teachings are a preparation to receive the gospel. Greek and Roman philosophy were not held equal to the Hebrew Scriptures in preparing people for Jesus, but this approach meant that classical culture was not altogether wasted if one were to become Christian. The *logos*, or

divine intelligence, to which the church claimed the fullest
access, was held to be present as a seed in the insights of
others.

Pagan philosophies continued to be influential in the
fourth century even after the emperor Constantine's recognition of Christianity. Roman culture did not become Christian overnight. But by the time of emperor Justinian in the
fifth century, Christianity felt few challenges from paganism. After the rise of Islam in the seventh century, the
church's rhetoric against pagans was not the prime concern.
What was left of paganism in the European Middle Ages
was at the level of local cult survivals, of folk customs,
especially in northern Europe. Some pagan customs were
adopted as harmless (such as the Yule log and other
seasonal, nontheological activities around Christmas), and
some were dismissed as superstition. Paganism had ceased
to be an intellectual rival of Christianity. From the time of
the Renaissance onward, classical civilization could be
admired without fear. Its architecture and literature could
serve as models for European styles, and names such as
Diana could be acceptable "Christian" names.

The question of paganism became a vital one once again
for European Christianity after the fifteenth century. The
age of exploration and trade brought Europeans into contact
with, and awarness of, civilizations that had high cultures,
such as those of India, China, and Japan. To these people
the gospel had seemingly never been preached (although
Syrian Christianity had reached both India and China by
late antiquity). One could not apply to Hindus, Confucians,
or Buddhists the arguments about validity of prophecy that
were used in disputes with Judaism or Islam. Yet their
teachings could not convincingly be dismissed as mere
superstition or witchcraft like the earlier religion of northern Europe.

Among Christians, Roman Catholics rather than Protestants led the way in reflecting on the faith of newly
discovered peoples, since Catholic Spain and Portugal

pioneered in the first phases of overseas exploration. In general, the church's position was that these peoples had an implicit faith which served as a "preparation" for the gospel.

To our own times the theme of "preparation" has dominated Catholic thinking about the non-Christian religions. A leading twentieth-century exponent of this view has been Karl Rahner, whose use of the term "anonymous Christians" has found wide currency. The brunt of the message is that Hindus, for example, are to a certain extent Christians already—without their knowing about it. This position holds that God, through his grace, is using the other religions to bring people to himself. Christ comes, unknown, to the Buddhist and the Hindu, who are oblivious to his coming and to the necessity of faith in him for salvation. But no matter; in this view, God in his grace is preparing them to receive Christ.

Today the question of other religions is a pressing one, partly because the dominant Protestant and Catholic views of recent decades have not proved adequate to what we now know of the religions. Barth's tension between human religion and God-given faith, popular among Protestants, simply does not ring true, for too many of us are aware of limitations in our own faith tradition or of the depth and richness of other faiths. Meanwhile, Rahner's reliance on the anonymity of grace to "baptize" the faith of others without their knowing it, popular among Catholics, is likewise unrealistic, for too many of us are aware that *we* could just as well be considered anonymous *Buddhists*, and that alleged Christians who do not profess the name of Christ are not very impressive as a church. A theological view of religions suitable for the decades to come will simply have to take a more adequate account of our plural, and pluralistic, world.

3
PLURALISM AND EVANGELISM

On a typical morning, I use an electric shaver from Holland, put on a shirt from Korea, eat breakfast off dishes from Great Britain with a fork from Japan, drive to work in a Swedish car, and sit down at a German typewriter. In our day, there is nothing particularly unusual about this. Manufactured goods as well as raw materials are shipped everywhere, and increasing numbers of corporations are operating in the international market.

It is not only material goods but also people and ideas that today move from continent to continent. Many of us have neighbors who have migrated from some other country, in some cases halfway around the world. Many of us have traveled overseas. And we have appropriated from elsewhere some quite exotic cultural items: the *idea* of simplicity that is implied in Japanese flower arranging, the *idea* of self-control that is implied in Indian yoga. Not everything "foreign" is attractive to us, but much is, and we find it readily compatible with our traditional ways. There is hardly a raised eyebrow when a church group does flower arranging or yoga.

"ONE WORLD"

Our world today, not surprisingly, is cosmopolitan. We often say this, but what do we mean by it? There are at least two factors in cosmopolitanism: first, intercultural contact and communication; and second, the self-conscious *awareness* of that contact.

No one doubts that we are in an interconnected world today. What we may not fully realize is the extent to which the world's cultures have been interconnected in the past. From the dawn of recorded history—a dawn we can place very close to 3000 B.C. because of the invention of writing at that time in Mesopotamia and Egypt—the Mediterranean Sea and the Indian Ocean served as avenues for long-distance maritime trade. We know from archaeology that by the second millennium B.C., the Mesopotamians were in contact with the Indus Valley culture of India, and the Canaanites were in touch with Greece. In the first millennium B.C. the Phoenicians got to the western Mediterranean from Lebanon, and Carthage (in Tunisia) began as a Phoenician ("Punic") colony. The Greco-Roman world traded directly with India and indirectly with China. In the Middle Ages, Arab navigators called at the ports of both, while overland commerce flourished along the "Silk Road," a central Asian trade route named for its principal westbound commodity.

The Rise of the West (1963), a stimulating world history by William H. McNeill, treats world history not in terms of the Middle Eastern to Mediterranean to North Atlantic pedigree that most standard histories in English use. McNeill concerns himself instead with the interaction of major empires and cultures strung one after another around the Eurasian continent. These were in touch with each other, with parallel achievements and mutual influences. They also had common problems, such as the pressure of nomadic populations, so-called "barbarians," from the interior of this huge land mass. What McNeill's book makes abundantly clear is the comparatively equal situation of these civilizations until the rise of modern Europe after 1500, when Western technology and culture began to dominate the world.

Perhaps the widespread or popular awareness of the interconnectedness of the world is a relatively modern phenomenon, but it is clear that even in ancient times there were those who thought of the unity of the known world as an intellectual and moral goal. Some even made it a political objective. Outstanding in this respect was the Greek-speaking ruler Alexander the Great, in the late fourth century B.C. Alexander, coming from the Mediterranean, took over the "known world" of the Persians and pushed on to northwestern India. A legend tells that he wept when he reached the Indus River, because there were no more worlds to conquer; that, of course, was a parochially Mediterranean view of the Asian continent. But Alexander was motivated by a dream of the unity of humanity. To the Greek world of Alexander's day we owe the term *oikoumene*, "inhabited world," from which comes our word "ecumenical."

What Alexander dreamed of has come much closer to realization twenty-four centuries later. Many problems in this century have become world problems, and are recognized as such: economics, ecology, disease control, crime, repression, and terrorism, to name a few. World institutions such as the United Nations have probably not been given enough support to cope with these problems. Few, however, would doubt the need for such organizations.

Do all peoples have a sense of the oneness of humanity? This is an interesting question, since the idea of a universal humanity may not necessarily be universally held. All cultures, it would seem, distinguish human beings from animals—from the "other" animals, perhaps we should say. It is not so clear that every culture is interested in the totality of the human race to quite the same extent. The anthropologist Kenelm Burridge, in *Encountering Aborigines* (1973), a book devoted to the specific case of Australian aboriginal cultures, makes the provocative point that European culture has shown an openness to, and curiosity about, other cultures that is unusual and perhaps even unique. If

Burridge is right, then cosmopolitanism may still have an unfinished job ahead to establish itself more firmly in the world.

SECULARISM

Christians today may find the ideal of human solidarity attractive, but it may grow from secular rather than religious roots. One element in secularism is an inherently positive valuation of humanity, a valuation which overlaps what is often termed "humanism." "Man is the measure of all things," the Greek philosophers put it. Following them, throughout more than two millennia of Western intellectual history, many have spoken optimistically about the capacity of people for right action, for knowledge, and for aesthetic creativity: for "the good, the true, and the beautiful."

Another element in secularism is an inherently negative stance toward domains of authority or even power beyond humanity. The term "secularism" does not always imply the denial of transcendent power in the universe altogether; but it does generally imply that there is an area of human life in which transcendent authority and values are irrelevant. Secularism tends to postulate two spheres: one in which religious institutions operate, and the other (the secular) in which they do not.

Part of the distinctiveness of the Western (Christian) sense of things is the duality of its heritage, which one could express metaphorically as the legacies of Mt. Sinai and Mt. Olympus. That is, as Christianity accommodated itself to classical culture, it recognized two sources of its heritage; the Hebraic tradition of revelation and the Hellenic philosophical tradition. In one sense, faith came from Jerusalem, and reason from Athens. (To the extent that there were nonrational or irrational elements in ancient Greece, Christendom conveniently forgot about them.) In the Middle Ages, both faith and reason were claimed

intellectually by the church, but the institutional distinction between the religious sphere of the church and the
secular sphere of kings and princes remained. A biblical
warrant for such a distinction was found in the instruction
of Jesus to render to Caesar what is Caesar's but to God
what is God's.

One of the hallmarks of modern life as it has emerged in
European history is the intellectual and institutional challenge to the authority of the church. From the Renaissance
through the Enlightenment, a revival of interest in the
Greek philosophical tradition offered alternative sources of
authority. The freedom of the individual was seen as a
release from the authority of both religious and political
institutions. Religious freedom and political freedom went
hand in hand, because European political and religious
institutions had long been seen as collaborating with one
another. The notion of individual religious liberty emerged
as an important part of the United States Constitution at the
end of the eighteenth century. What emerged in the United
States, and was likewise a factor in the French revolution,
was the principle of the separation of church and state.

In the United States this principle has applied not only to
religious worship but also to religious instruction. The
chief support which religious bodies have received from
various levels of government has been exemption from
taxation; but after 1962 the academic study of religion grew
rapidly. A major feature of that growth was the study of the
major world religions critically and comparatively as a
human phenomenon. Secularism opposes religious indoc-
trination, and encourages a critical stance by the academic
observer. This stance would in principle be independent of
commitment to any particular religious tradition.

PLURALISM

There are two essential aspects to the idea of pluralism: a
fact and an evaluation. In today's society of migration,

travel, and multiple influences, plurality is an evident fact. Pluralism is the endorsement of this fact: the view that plurality is a desirable thing. This positive evaluation, this acceptance of diversity, in its turn becomes a fact. It is this second fact, the religious pluralism of our contemporary society, that is one of the principal concerns of contemporary theology, and of this book.

Prior to World War II, American pluralism was a largely interdenominational Christian phenomenon. The entry of Judaism into the mainstream of American religious life was well-nigh complete by 1955, when Will Herberg's book *Protestant—Catholic—Jew* appeared Herberg documented what had come to seem self-evident at least to younger people by that date: Judaism was one of the three principal and co-equal religious options in "this Christian land of ours." Mutual acceptance was becoming firmly enshrined as an American ideal, as part of the American way of life. Herberg also alerted us to the value placed on religiosity per se, or as he called it, America's faith in faith itself.

There are two important implications of the principle of pluralism. One is its challenge to missionary activity. If diversity is inherently desirable, then what right do we have to go out and try to convert others to our faith? What right do we have to try to convert a Jewish neighbor, for instance? Christian evangelistic work aimed at Jews continues in some quarters, but since World War II it has been emphatically curtailed by the mainline denominations. I recall discussing world religions with the faculty of the Yale Divinity School during the 1960s, arguing for a deeper theological appreciation of other religions. In the course of the discussion I asked how many would support an effort to convert Jews to Christianity, and not one—not a single one—of the assembled theologians would express such a wish. Some were willing to support overseas missions among adherents of other traditions, but all could give

theological or practical reasons for pluralism when it came
to Jewish identity.

A second implication of pluralism is its emphasis on
representation. Civic committees, boards, and the like must
have Protestant, Catholic, and Jewish members. A pluralistic society tends to operate on the equal-time principle: that
is, each group gets a chance to state its own views. The
pluralist approach to interreligious description often requires that a speaker from a religious community act as its
representative, and this dialogue of participants with ob-
servers where it has occurred has been a salutary thing for
both parties.

In summary, the social fact of plurality has forced the
social and intellectual attitude of pluralism. The consequences of pluralism for religious community are yet to be
weighed.

"Into All the World"

"As long as there has been religion, there have been
missionaries," it has been said. Certainly Christianity from
its very beginnings was a missionary faith. Its spread spans
several phases, which we can outline only briefly.

For its first three centuries, Christianity was a minority
religion (compare Islam, which was established during its
founder's lifetime as the religiopolitical order of a total
society). To be a Christian in the Roman Empire was at
times a very risky business. One became a Christian at great
potential personal sacrifice. People entered the church as a
deliberate act, sometimes in the face of social ostracism or
political persecution. Usually, one didn't just "happen" to
be Christian.

Although the kingdom of Armenia had been Christian
from the mid-third century, the conversion of Constantine
in the early fourth represents for us the shift of Christian
fortunes from persecution to patronage. Estimates of Con-

stantine's motives range all the way from pious convert to scheming opportunist. He may have undergone a gradual or a sudden change of personal loyalty to Christianity, or he may have simply found in the church's institutions the organization and discipline that he needed to stabilize an empire that had been near anarchy. In any event, his outward acts reflect a pattern of first toleration and then favor toward Christianity. Rome did not become Christian overnight, but by the end of the fourth century it was fairly solidly so.

For some centuries thereafter the principal expansion of Christianity consisted of the conversion of whole populations, often through a direct approach to their ruler or chieftain. Missions to the peoples of western and northern Europe resulted in a Christianization which survived the fall of the Empire in the Latin-speaking western Mediterranean. Similarly, Christian missions from the Greek-speaking Byzantine Empire spread Christianity among the Slavic peoples, so that Orthodox Christianity became the dominant form from the eastern Mediterranean and Balkans to Russia.

There were a few independent eastern Christian churches in Ethiopia, Egypt, Syria, Mesopotamia, India, and central Asia, but their expansion was halted after the seventh century by the spread of Islam, westward from Arabia across North Africa and eastward into central Asia. For eight centuries, throughout the Middle Ages, the Islamic world was a geographical barrier to the expansion of Christianity.

At the end of the fifteenth century, Europe's nearly simultaneous discoveries of the western hemisphere and the sea route around Africa opened up new avenues for the expansion of Christianity. The Spanish conquest of the Incas in Peru and the Aztecs and Mayas in Mexico left few living vestiges of these ancient cultures. In the Americas and in Africa, Christianization of the tribal populations continued, which resembled in some ways Christianity's

earlier spread in northern and eastern Europe, except that
here the Christians had the military and political power as
well.

Except for the Philippines, the missionary picture was
quite different throughout Asia. Here the European Christians were in contact with historic cultures and philosophically sophisticated traditions which showed little sign of
collapse. Centuries of European effort in India, China, and
Japan have produced only a small Christian minority in
these lands.

The most significant Christian missionary efforts after the
opening of European contact were undertaken by the
Jesuits. Saint Francis Xavier reached Goa, a Portuguese
colony on the west coast of India, in 1542, and went on to
Japan in 1549. By 1606 there were 750,000 Christians in
Japan, but persecution soon reduced the figures. Within
eighty years of Xavier's arrival Christianity had nearly
disappeared from Japan, as the Tokugawa regime sought to
seal off the country from foreign influences.

The Jesuits followed a different strategy in China. Under
Matteo Ricci and his able successors Adam Schall and
Ferdinand Verbiest, they began work in the middle of the
sixteenth century which was to last through the middle of
the eighteenth before its collapse. The Jesuits in China
found favor at the imperial court, attracting attention because of their skill in astronomy and clockmaking, but also
because of their attempt to state Christian ideas in the terms
of Confucian philosophy. Many of the mandarin elite became converts to Christianity, and the Jesuits for a consid-
erable time hoped to Christianize this vast society from the
top down. Christian influence in China was curtailed
through Rome's rulings in the "Rites Controversy," a late-
seventeenth-century dispute over the acceptability of missionary accommodation to Chinese tradition: ethical respect for Confucius; ceremonial veneration for the departed
ancestors, through prostrations, incense and food offerings,
and the like; and Christian equation of the idea of God with

certain terms in the Confucian classic texts, especially T'ien (Heaven) and Shang-ti (the Lord Above). There were of course exceptions to the picture, but by and large the Franciscans and Dominicans, who preached a rather clumsy rejection of Chinese culture, prevailed in influence at Rome. The losers were the Jesuits, with their careful efforts to integrate a Chinese Christianity with the indigenous cultural tradition. With the repudiation of the Jesuits, their dream for the Christianization of China became clearly unrealizable.

Nineteenth-century Protestantism in Europe and America also saw a massive outpouring of missionary energy. The Student Volunteer Movement is only one example of this. It drew strength from some Protestants' expectations of the second coming of Christ, with a consequent urge to complete the church's outreach before that event. With huge quadrennial missionary conventions over the years 1891 to 1919, the SVM recruited more than eight thousand missionaries. Evangelical Protestants, like the Franciscans in Asia, often stressed a rejection of old ways as a precondition for entering the promise of the new. The agenda of these missionaries, and what they sought to reject, was often confusing to the minds of their Asian and African audiences.

There was sometimes conflict between European entrepreneurs and colonial civil servants on the one hand and missionaries on the other, because of the activist role that missionaries from time to time took in opposing colonial policy. The British East India Company, seeking to ground its authority in the "ancient laws" of Indian tradition, was not interested in sudden changes in the allegiance of the people. It succeeded in excluding missionaries until 1813, when pressure in England for evangelism forced the company to open the doors to India. In 1895 Rudyard Kipling, whom we link with political imperialism, challenged the missionary rationale: it was cruel, he said, that white people should "confound their fellow creatures with a doctrine of salvation imperfectly understood by themselves and a code of ethics foreign to the climate and instinct of those races whose most cherished customs they outrage and whose gods they insult." Support for missionary activity even in its heyday in the Victorian era was not as uniform as later generations have sometimes pictured it to be.

RETHINKING MISSIONS

The word "missionary" has a positive as well as a negative significance. We speak of missionary zeal, a sense of dedicated self-sacrifice, as the altruistic desire to share one's belief with others. But today, especially in colonial or post-colonial lands, the word also suggests cultural and religious imperialism. Westerners in the nineteenth century frequently confronted peoples of different traditions with a smug statement of superiority. Westerners used both the carrot and the stick: they offered employment or other advantages to their converts (hence the term "rice Christians"), and they backed up their cultural and intellectual assaults not only with the promise of hellfire hereafter but with some very here-and-now gunboats. Thus the missionary's reputation is ambiguous: a self-invited guest who wishes to take over.

Are missions doing more harm than good? Must Christianity inevitably be a missionary religion? How else is one to interpret Matt. 28:19: "Go therefore and make disciples of all nations, baptizing them . . ."? In our century, the need to "re-think" missions has been felt urgently, particularly as several facts have come home to the churches in the Western world:

1. Newly independent nations are not eager, to say the least, for continued missionary campaigns sponsored by the former colonial powers. Western Christianity is seen as imperialist, and rejected as such.

2. The major world religions, notably Islam but also

Hinduism and Buddhism, have shown themselves remarkably resistant to efforts at conversion. Christianity must face the fact of minimal returns on a massive investment of money and talent, and it must ask whether continued efforts can be justified.

3. The nontheological aspects of mission, such as education, agriculture, village development, and medical work, have proven more successful than evangelistic mission. But these efforts are now being picked up by various national governments. The Christian colleges in many lands are no longer the most prestigious academic institutions.

4. Indigenous churches have become established in many lands and have taken over the efforts that used to be supported from outside. "Self-government, self-support, and self-propagation" were advocated by Rufus Anderson, a nineteenth-century American missionary leader, and the goal of indigenous self-sufficiency was shared by other missionaries. In the middle of the twentieth century, the Chinese Protestant church under Communist rule advocated this independence of outside influence, and called itself the Three-Self Movement.

5. Christians, especially in Africa, have contended that many forms of worship and norms of conduct brought by the Europeans are utterly alien to African ways of thinking. Rather than build on local tradition and "indigenize" the church, many Christians have preached a radical break with a pagan culture, a break which loses more support through alienation than it gains in theological purity. Could not the indigenous cultures function as a preparation for the Christian message as the Old Testament did for the earliest church?

6. Denominational divisions that may have had some historical or national explanation back in the missionary's home country have meant nothing but confusion on the mission field. What, for example, does it mean to be a Korean Southern Baptist, or a Japanese Lutheran of the Missouri Synod?

7. Christian exclusivism has not always had productive
results in local societies. Requiring a profession of Christian faith for access to Christian institutions has had the
negative result of producing hypocrisy among some who
affiliate for expediency and also resentment among those
excluded. A notable example is the Ugandan dictator Idi
Amin, who, as an able and ambitious young man, was
denied access to Christian educational opportunities, and
made his way up the only ladder open to him—a repressive
police career. Opportunities that have given some communities an exclusive advantage over others have sometimes
backfired against them.

Rethinking missions is not new. In 1932, it was the title of
a book-length report of an American Protestant Laymen's
Foreign Missions Inquiry, written by the committee's
chairman, the liberal Harvard philosopher William Ernest
Hocking. Hocking's book raised many questions and stirred
a widespread debate. The Barthian theologian Hendrik
Kraemer, a veteran of the Dutch Reformed mission field in
Indonesia, countered with *The Christian Message in a Non-
Christian World* (1938). Hocking's stress on human univer-
sals versus Kraemer's emphasis on uniquely revealed particulars constituted a classic confrontation within the
church of these two divergent emphases, which it has
known throughout most of its two millennia. If we feel
guilty about our attempts to intrude into others' lives and
cultures, and if we are not getting results anyway, why
continue missions? And yet, if we have experienced the
truth and Christ has commanded us to preach it, what
choice have we?

Recent decades have seen little by way of breakthrough
in the "whether or not" question with regard to missions
but have seen a certain amount of development with
respect to "how." The missionary's role is seen as a partici-
pant in another church and another culture, as a co-laborer
rather than a "spiritual foreman." And local political conditions in the host countries have contributed to a degree of

institutional indigenization that the mission boards back
home have had to accept; to some extent this has encouraged a more subtle process of cultural indigenization as
well. Each generation, perhaps, must rethink its rationale of
mission as well as the means to implement it.

ON THE RECEIVING END

Other religions are missionary too. In recent times, Christianity has felt the impact of mission activity by major Asian
traditions, as well as more specific sects.

Of course, the biggest single impact of another religion in
the Christian world occurred fourteen centuries ago: the
spread of Islam. But Islam spread more through conquest
than through what we normally think of as missionary
activity.

In recent centuries Islamic missions have been active in
Africa. While Christians arrived in the ports along the west
coast of Africa and worked their way up the rivers, Islam
was making its way along the inland trade routes of the
southern edge of the Sahara. On the east coast of Africa,
meanwhile, both Islam and Christianity arrived by sea. In
both East and West Africa, the two religions have found
each other competing for the allegiance of tribal peoples.
To many, the simplicity of Islamic doctrine has been more
appealing than Christianity. Muslims, moreover, have been
able to avoid identification with European imperialism,
even though it was Islamic powers in the Gulf area that had
been involved in the East African slave trade. Some observ-
ers have commented that Islam has succeeded better than
Christianity in adapting its practices to local tribal custom.

Buddhism is the world's third great missionary religion.
Its missionary spread from India to southeast Asia and to
China two thousand years ago led to Buddhism's survival,
since within India itself it was absorbed into the medieval
Indian tradition. But Buddhism's big impact has been

recent. It was due to the intellectual influence of Daisetz T. Suzuki, who lived in the United States in the twentieth century, that Zen teachings and discipline were popularized among Americans looking for alternatives to Western modes of reflection and theories of personal consciousness. By the mid-1960s, few could be considered educated who did not have at least a vague idea of Zen, even if it amounted only to a stand-up comedian's characterization of it as "a kind of philosophical-metaphysical-thought thing."

What has made the question of Asian missionaries to the West a pressing one is not so much Zen, however, as certain movements that have reached North America and Europe, notably from India. The new religious groups, or "cults" as they are often popularly called, frequently attractive to young people in their teens and twenties, present a phenomenon of near-absolute commitment to their teaching and regimen, often coupled with a severing of contact with family and former friends. One of the most misleading things that one can do is to suppose that all of the new religious groups are just the same, even if they do show some psychosocial similarities in the role they give to group solidarity.

Many of the young people who join the new religious groups are highly idealistic, motivated by a desire to improve society. They may also be alienated from their parents, little appreciated by their own families, and thus seeking a "family" substitute. In some cases, too, it has been shown that the homes from which the new religious group members came were both prosperous and permissive. "I gave my daughter everything she wanted," is a recurring complaint. "What wrong could I have possibly done her? What else could she possibly want?" The question contains its own answer: the wrong was to give her everything—except a discipline. Many have been drawn to the new religious groups from affluent homes precisely because of the discipline or sacrifice the groups have demanded.

These new religious groups include those with roots in Hinduism, such as Transcendental Meditation, the International Society for Krishna Consciousness (Hare Krishna), and Ananda Marga; 3HO or "Sikh Dharma" is another Indian religion. Two other widely known groups with Western origins are the Church of Scientology and the Children of God, while the Holy Spirit Association for the Unification of World Christianity (the Unification Church or "Moonies"), founded by a Korean, is perhaps the most widely publicized of the so-called "new religions."

Taken as a whole, the new religious groups, whether of Asian or Western origin, Hindu or Christian, pose a set of ethical and legal problems to the Christian West. What, after all, are the limits of religious freedom? Is there any criterion of substance or of doctrine by which some groups might be branded fraudulent? Is there any criterion of behavior by which some groups might be branded coercive? The problem is, quite simply, that many of the things that are characteristic of the new religious groups—chanting, discipline, self-sacrificing loyalty, active proselytizing—were equally characteristic of the early Christian church in its first missionary outreach. These features still characterize certain movements, particularly Catholic religious orders, in mainline Christendom. If legislatures were to prescribe or courts to describe the acceptable content of religion, it would mark a radical departure from our ideals of freedom and our concept of a pluralistic society. It may be that our Western laws may only restrain overt political rebellion, overt fiscal fraud, or overt coercion. Traditional Christianity may have to live out its golden rule in the presence of new missionary movements, giving them the liberty that one would seek for one's own missionary outreach.

4
GROUND RULES FOR DIALOGUE

Our world has made interreligious dialogue a more pressing issue than it has been in previous centuries. But what do we mean by dialogue, and what is the current state of interreligious dialogue?

DIALOGUE IN THE PAST

Some recent Christian writers on interreligious dialogue have started with a textual approach to the subject. These authors trace the word "dialogue" back to its linguistic roots and to its usage in classic texts. "Dialogue" is from a Greek word meaning to argue, to reason, or to contend. A frequently cited text is Acts 19:8–9, where Paul is in Ephesus "arguing and pleading about the kingdom of God." Paul is involved daily in putting the Christian case to his audience, both in the synagogue at Ephesus and in the Greek philosophical school of Tyrannus. Dialogue, by this precedent, consists of debate or disputation, designed to win over people to one's own view. The text goes on to suggest that Paul was very successful at it, and won both Jews and non-Jews in Asia Minor to Christianity.

If evangelistic preaching, and more particularly, the kind of rational argument in favor of one's own view that we call apologetics, is what "dialogue" means, then history abounds with examples of such argumentation. This was the burden of most dialogue situations in past eras, but today the meaning of "dialogue" has shifted in a significant way. What is meant by interfaith dialogue today is a far cry from the interreligious attitudes of past centuries.

As literature, the dialogue form has always been a report of conversations and exchanges of argument. A few reported dialogues may represent actual conversations, but most are imagined. They represent schools of thought rather than being tape-recorded transcripts. The Greek philosopher Plato set forth his own views and those of his mentor, Socrates, in writings in which those who raise objections come off sometimes as naive and sometimes as profound but always as swimming in vain against the tide of Socrates' (or Plato's) logic. Similarly, the Upanishads (a name meaning "sessions"), which are discourses on ancient Indian religious philosophy, are cast in dialogue form but are clearly composed to advance an argument. And the early Christian apologist Justin Martyr carried on "dialogues" with the Jew Trypho. None of these literary dialogues was, in the mind of its author, really open with respect to the ultimate outcome.

Literary dialogues are not limited to bygone ages. The eighteenth-century French Enlightenment philosopher Nicolas Malebranche wrote *Entretien d'un philosophe chrétien et un philosophe chinois,* in which a Christian debates with a Chinese Confucian. The Christian wins the logical arguments, principally because the form of Christianity presented accords with Malebranche's rationalist ideas. The Confucian philosophy is seen as reflecting, sometimes clearly and sometimes more faintly, the insights of Christianity. "Ah," the Christian says in effect, "I see that your idea of *li* [cosmic principle] approaches our idea of God."

It is characteristic of apologetic works, whether written in dialogue form or not, to be more forgiving toward the symbolic statements of the author's own tradition than toward those of another. An embarrassing anthropomorphism in one's own heritage can be dismissed as "mere" symbolism, whereas in somebody else's tradition it can be criticized as evidence of a fundamental naïveté. People tend to read their own traditions liberally and others' traditions literally.

The premodern literature was polemical. It aimed at converting the reader by demolishing the arguments of the opposition. "Dialogue" may have been the form, but conquest rather than understanding was the objective. Genuine, open efforts, in which the outcome was not foreclosed or predetermined, stand out as exceptions.

One premodern exception that deserves mention took place in the court of late sixteenth-century northern India, under the leadership of the Mughal emperor Akbar. Akbar was a Muslim who ruled a diverse population, predominantly Hindu but also including Sikhs, Christians, Zoroastrians, and others. Convinced of the need for harmony within his realm, Akbar summoned representatives of the various communities to his court and conducted what amounted to seminars in the comparative study of religion.

Akbar not only sought to demonstrate in discussion the essential unity of the various religious traditions of his realm, but eventually he made this claim an article of faith. In 1582 he proclaimed the Din-i-ilahi, "Divine Faith," an eclectic amalgam which, however well intentioned, did not catch on outside the circles of his court or last after his death. Bada'uni, a later Muslim historian critical of Akbar, wrote that "persons of novel and whimsical opinions . . . decked the false in the garb of the true, and wrong in the dress of right, and cast the emperor . . . into perplexity, till doubt was heaped upon doubt, and he lost all definite aim . . . so that after five or six years not a trace of Islam was left in him: and everything was turned topsy-turvy." For traditional religions, disputation has been one thing, and welcome when one is in control of the outcome. But Akbar's was something else, open-ended rather than closed. Open dialogue, a dialogue between or among equals and open to the possibility of reciprocal influence and change, has been inherently uncontrollable and therefore potentially threatening to those already committed to a fixed position.

THE EMERGENCE OF DIALOGUE TODAY

The modern era in interreligious relationships has been in evidence for about a century. In 1892 at the Columbian Exposition in Chicago—the four-hundredth anniversary of the "discovery" of the New World by Columbus—a Presbyterian minister, John H. Barrows, decided to promote and convene a World's Parliament of Religions. In 1893, religious leaders came to Chicago from all over the world to speak about what their own traditions taught and to celebrate what each religion contributed to human unity and human progress. This Parliament had lasting effects. It introduced Vedanta (Hindu monistic philosophy) to American intellectual audiences, and gave Vedanta a head start toward becoming the most representative form of Hinduism in the minds of Westerners. It also introduced the Baha'i faith to the western hemisphere. Baha'i had started as a Shi'ite sectarian movement in nineteenth-century Iran. After its rebellion had failed, its exiled leaders found that outside Iran there was a market for a transformation of Baha'i into a synthesizing overview of various religious prophets and teachings as a divinely ordained succession. The world in 1893 was becoming increasingly cosmopolitan, ready to try out new teachings and explore new syntheses.

Neither Akbar's court in sixteenth-century India nor the World's Parliament of Religions in nineteenth-century America constituted dialogue as it is known today. The essential difference between these past symposia and some of the best recent efforts is that the Christian communities involved in dialogue today are actually entering into con-

versation with other communities *as communities*. The
participants want to make a common statement on matters
of mutual concern and with the possibility of modifying the
Christian stand on one topic or another in the light of the
negotiation with, or understanding of, another religious
group.

This has seldom happened before. It is clear, for instance,
that Akbar spoke neither for the rank and file of Muslims
nor for most Hindus when he proclaimed his eclectic faith.
Barrows spoke for the liberal sentiments of many individual
Christians when he envisioned an era of brotherhood and
peace at the Chicago parliament, but it is clear that he did
not speak for any denomination, even his own, on the
question of exclusive and final claims to truth.

It is not that the twentieth-century communities *as communities* have yet altered their claims to exclusive and final
truth. Formally and officially, their theological positions
remain largely what they have been through the centuries.
What has happened, however, particularly within the past
generation or two, is that Christian groups have agreed to
disagree with others with respect to their truth claims while
actively seeking ground for common endeavor on practical
matters.

One big factor is social concern. By overwhelming odds,
the most common interfaith contact in North American
society is the interaction between Christians and Jews.
Interaction has of course been high at the individual level.
Especially in the urban areas of the American Northeast
and Midwest, and on the Pacific Coast, Christians and Jews
have lived, worked, and studied side by side. They have
seen their towns and cities grow and change, and change
has not always been for the better. As people with religious
values, and with a sense of human unity, they have often
talked individually concerning civic welfare and public
policy. Jewish and Christian neighbors could often agree
on liberal social causes, such as support for improved
educational or health facilities, even if their misperceptions

of each other's religious tenets were more of a hindrance than a starting point for conversation.

It is no wonder, therefore, that some of the strongest links between Jews and Christians in North America during the first half of the century were formed in the public policy arena, and that formal organizational contacts at the local level have been the most extensive. To be sure, a certain amount of the collaboration of rabbis and Christian clergy at the level of local ministerial councils and institutional chaplaincies has been toward maintaining the rights of religious groups and personnel in relation to public institutions. But what has more significantly enlisted the dedication of laity and clergy alike has been a shared address toward community problems: prejudice, race relations, and the like. Jews made common cause with Christians in the early 1960s in the civil rights struggle for dignity for American blacks. So long as matters were practical and domestic, the alliance worked well. On international questions, which are a more complicated story, differences emerged, and these will be discussed later.

At the local level, there has been relatively little interfaith conversation between Christians and groups other than the Jews—with Muslims, or Hindus, or Sikhs. In North America these contacts are more recent than Christian-Jewish ones. Significant immigration from India and Southeast Asia has occurred largely since World War II, and it has been concentrated mainly in certain urban centers.

I live in Toronto, which must be one of the most fascinating living laboratories in intergroup perception anywhere. Toronto has doubled in radius and quadrupled in population in the past generation, notably through immigration. An estimated one million Torontonians—40 percent of the city—were born outside Canada, giving Toronto today probably the highest proportion of foreign-born residents of any major city in the world. With horizons formerly limited to Canada's French-English duality, the province of Ontario now promotes multiculturalism, and its Christian denom-

inations participate in an active concern to promote a
positive spirit in society and combat prejudice. Interfaith
bodies—including their national offices as well as their
local chapters—find that the most meaningful achievement
to which they can point is not necessarily some conference
of specialists halfway around the world but often a tangible
program of local family and neighborhood contact.

Such contact, everyone hopes, will overcome some of the
prejudices about Asian and Middle Eastern religions that
persist in a still Christian-dominated society. If a Hindu, for
example, is taunted in a public place, or if a Sikh is required
by a local health or dress regulation to trim his hair or
beard, other religious communities can lend support. If a
Muslim family moves into the neighborhood, an organized
program of family-to-family exchanges or gatherings can
help the non-Muslims to understand the new neighbors'
reluctance to drink alcohol or to allow girls to go unchaper-
oned. Clearly, one main emphasis of intergroup efforts must
be education, since it is principally through ignorance that
prejudice is perpetuated.

Although the practical realm is where much of the local
success has been achieved, many local efforts in Christian-
Jewish or other contacts have also sought to assume or to
demonstrate a shared intellectual and spiritual heritage. In
some cases the assumption of similarity has proved naive
and has overlooked basic differences. Some Jews, indeed,
object to the presumed equation in the expression "Judeo-
Christian tradition." Christians have—understandably, of
course—sought to understand other religions in Christian
terms rather than looking for the distinctive categories of
the others' own self-understanding. It sometimes requires
technical or scholarly knowledge, coupled with the experience gleaned from previous occasions of dialogue, to deal
responsibly with the major outstanding issues.

The expertise that is required has been accumulating at
the national and international levels. During the twentieth
century an awareness of the need for dialogue has become

more widespread in the World Council of Churches (representing Protestant and Eastern Orthodox bodies) and the
Roman Catholic Church. The World Council of Churches'
antecedents are commonly traced to Protestant collaboration from 1910 onward in youth work and especially in
overseas missions. The historic Christian divisions, which
accounted for the separate identities of Protestant denominations, continued to mean something in the European
context and may have meant something among the descendants of Europeans settled in North America; but it
was the overwhelming recognition of workers in the Asian
and African mission field that such historic divisions had
little to say to the non-Western world. Collaboration on the
Asian Christian mission scene between the two world wars,
together with the maturing of the younger leadership in this
movement, led to the formation of the World Council of
Churches following World War II.

The insights of Protestant ecumenism included a sense of
common creed and common purpose: confession of Jesus
Christ as Lord and a calling to bear witness in a secular and
strife-torn world. What Protestant ecumenism also learned
was a style of conversation and spirit of mutual acceptance
on which concerted action could be based. Protestants
could agree to act together in missions, in international
affairs and refugee relief, and in a host of other practical
areas, even when questions of "faith and order" remained
unresolved. Branches of Protestant Christianity that had
been separated for four centuries could agree on the need
for world peace but in some cases could not find ways to
recognize each other's ordination as valid or eucharistic
communion as sharable. The church doctrine and church
order of earlier centuries, in short, were dragged kicking
and screaming into the twentieth century by practical
realities and the need for community.

What Protestants learned in the ecumenical movement
was the preservation of diversity within unity. The
churches were indeed united on many points; yet nobody

denied the differences that remained. Their separate identities were not reduced to the lowest common denominator.
Protestants developed a respectful appreciation of diversity, and an earnest desire to appreciate the distinctiveness of
varying traditions. The fears of assimilation that some had
at the time of the World Council's establishment in 1948
were amply dispelled during the 1950s. Alongside its
confident address to practical matters of public concern, a
style of dialogue emerged on matters of faith and order in
the Council; Christians agreed to disagree and listened to
one another's agendas.

In the 1950s official Roman Catholic participation in the
then pan-Protestant ecumenical movement would have
seemed a utopian dream. Rome, after all, had little patience
for Protestants, holding them to be in error and stipulating
that any reconciliation of the sixteenth-century split in
Christendom would have to be on Rome's terms. But the
career of John XXIII changed all that almost overnight.
Coming to the papacy in 1959, John called for *aggiorna-
mento* (updating) in the Roman Catholic Church, and he
convoked the Second Vatican Council to achieve it.

Vatican II meant a transformation of the idea of pan-
Christian ecumenism from a dream to a reality. From the
1960s onward, little could be called truly ecumenical which
did not include Catholics as well as Protestants and Orthodox Christians. In everything from civil rights marches to
theological education, Catholics began to sit and to work
beside their "separated brethren." Centuries of Protestant-
Catholic prejudice began to dissipate more rapidly than
anyone who had grown up before the 1960s could have
expected. One measure of the advance that Christian ecumenism made is the extent to which, when strife broke out
between Catholics and Protestants in Northern Ireland in
1969, leaders of both traditions elsewhere sought to dissociate themselves from the politics of their Irish coreligionists
and to indicate that the Northern Irish conflict ran counter
to the spirit of both Catholic and Protestant Christianity.

It was but a simple step, and a logical one, to proceed from the agenda of intra-Christian ecumenism to the question of relationships with other religions. The Second Vatican Council did this, bringing forth *Nostra Aetate,* the Declaration on the Relation of the Church to Non-Christian Religions. In fact, in the politics of the Council, there was a certain degree of tension between those (especially in Europe) who wanted to make a statement apologizing for Christendom's medieval and modern wrongs against the Jews, and others (especially in the Middle East) who held that a pro-Jewish statement, if not balanced by a concern for Islam and the other world religions, would be detrimental to the situation of Christians in Muslim lands, especially Arab Christians. There was also positive support for a wide-ranging declaration, rather than a merely Christian-Jewish one, on the part of Catholic leaders who were serving, or had served, in South and East Asia. This support contributed to the development of a Vatican Secretariat for Non-Christians, whose work has continued in the decades since the Council.

The World Council of Churches and its intra-Christian ecumenism owed much to the experience of Christians in Asia, where European differences appeared irrelevant. The World Council's involvement in "the wider ecumenism" is likewise indebted to voices from Asia—this time because Christians as a minority there are daily exposed to the major world religions. Informal dialogue for a Christian in a land such as India is not a luxury but an everyday occurrence.

Barthian theology flourished in the decades just before and after World War II. As long as this line of reasoning held sway, dialogue on equal terms among the religious communities was hardly possible. In the report on the 1954 assembly of the World Council, General Secretary W. A. Visser 't Hooft wrote, "It is not so much the truth of these systems of thought and feeling which makes appeal, but rather the present determination to interpret and change oppressive conditions of life." The practical concern of public policy in newly independent countries was to many Europeans a more important reason for talking than the appreciation of a non-Christian doctrine. A study of "The Word of God and the Living Faiths of Men" was launched by the World Council, and by the time of its next assembly in 1961 the matter of dialogue was commended to local study centers; but it did not yet receive a central place in the thinking of the World Council.

A statement from the East Asia Christian Conference (Bangkok, 1964) spurred a response which, coming at about the same time as the Second Vatican Council, began to stir Protestant interfaith relations out of their Barthian slumbers. The action was, predictably, in Asia. A consultation on "Christians in Dialogue with Men of Other Faiths" was held in Sri Lanka in 1967, with Roman Catholic scholars included for the first time. The World Council added to its central staff for studies in the dialogue field. In 1970, in Lebanon, a conference under World Council auspices was held for the first time with representatives of various religions. This was no longer a study of dialogue but was an example of it.

The pace quickened in the 1970s, as bilateral and multilateral dialogues flourished and literature on the practice and techniques of dialogue began to proliferate. The pamphlet *Guidelines on Dialogue*, summarizing some findings, appeared in 1979. In the World Council's organizational restructuring of 1971, the unit on Dialogue with People of Living Faiths and Ideologies was given a status on a level with such standard and central concerns as Faith and Order, Church and Society, and World Mission and Evangelism. Dialogue—a two-way exchange as distinct from earlier one-way notions of witness—had come of age.

PRINCIPLES OF DIALOGUE

Dialogue entails an attempt, first of all, to understand another tradition for its own sake and in its own terms.

Inescapably, this means putting an end to deliberate misrepresentation and distortion of the position of one's dialogue partner. For centuries interreligious polemic—not just polemic by Christians but by others as well—consisted of portraying the opponent's views as defective or ridiculous. The aim, of course, was to score points in a competitive debate. Comparisons are odious indeed when one compares the shortcomings and sufferings of a society such as India's with the teachings of Jesus; no one denies that the ideals of the gospel would improve the life of the world. But European and American society also falls far short of the Christian ideal and would also profit from a dose of the gospel. It is a cardinal sin in the comparison of religious traditions and communities to compare the ideals of one's own with the achievements of another. As the World Council guidelines have put it, the Christian warrant or injunction for refraining from deliberate distortion of others is the commandment: "You shall not bear false witness against your neighbor."

Even when the attempt is not to distort or even to score points, the conduct of Christians and the vocabulary we choose may have an unintended distorting effect. We talk of dialogue with "non-Christians," for example; this is indeed the designation of the Vatican Secretariat for that purpose. Factually, the designation "non-Christian" is accurate enough. But is it either fair or useful for the purposes of understanding? If you were a Buddhist, do you think "non-Christian" would describe your identity? (All it would describe would be your status in the eyes of another society.) Would a Christian think that the adjective "non-Buddhist" would describe the central features of Christian identity? When the shoe is on the other foot, we can feel the pinch.

One goal for dialogue must be an understanding of the partner's identity in itself and for its own sake. Christians have been noticeably guilty on this score when it comes to understanding Judaism. We tend to assume that our own tradition, with its own notions of scriptural interpretation, salvation or redemption, and the like, is the standard against which another is to be measured. Urging awareness of the other in the other's own terms, I wrote (in *Theology Today*, 1966), "It is little short of scandalous that American seminary graduates can be considered educated without having been asked to understand contemporary Jewish faith." A friend in the Judaica field who read that article replied, in a letter: "That's great, Will. And I would respond that it is likewise scandalous that rabbinical students are not asked to have a knowledge of the New Testament and early Christianity, so important for an understanding of the Talmud." To understand the Talmud? He had missed the point completely. It is not only Christians who make their own tradition the primary object of understanding; it is a temptation to our partners as well.

Yet we cannot eliminate our own tradition from the business of understanding. After all, the most common way to understand anything is to associate it with something we know already. Confucius is a figure "like Socrates," we might say, and in so saying we have managed to make sense of his role as a teacher or his sense of justice in society. Ashoka is "like Constantine," in that he made his faith the official religion of his empire. Our minds skip across the lines separating communities and cultures, and we discern common patterns. A priest, a temple, a ritual, a sacrifice, a prayer, perhaps a scripture: these categories and many more we draw from our own tradition and identify resemblances with them. Indeed, some of the most influential writing on Christian understanding of Islam in the past generation has taken key similarities as the starting points for understanding: for example, the Islamic notion of ingratitude and the Christian notions of pride and sin.

If we are going to understand others at all, we must start with our own terminology because that is all we have. Understanding is like building a bridge, with a foundation on each side. Or to use another simile, it is like translation from one vocabulary to another. Part of the experience of dialogue and of religious scholarship during recent decades is that when we use our own institutions and ideas and vocabulary as a starting point, we must look for the limitations of that vocabulary. We must look for the differences as well as the similarities. The sacred river of the Hindus, the Ganges, is a river like the Jordan; yet any responsible Christian understanding of Hinduism will seek to note the ways in which the Ganges is a river unlike the Jordan. Or, to take another example, the Buddhist notion of contemplation runs temptingly parallel to the Christian mystics' notion of deeply felt union with God; but to generalize about "mysticism" or to understand either its Buddhist or Christian forms, it is equally imperative to know how Buddhist contemplation is unlike the Christian.

As a process of understanding, dialogue obliges us to challenge and if necessary revise our received and preconceived ideas about our partners. To be able to do this, we must enter into the process with an openness to change: a willingness to be changed by the encounter, not merely a dedication to change others. True dialogue has risks, and requires that participants be at peace with themselves and their own communities. Such self-acceptance is an essential foundation for the mutual acceptance, the sharing of a common world, a common life, and common causes, to which interfaith and intercommunal dialogue points today.

SPECIFIC AGENDA ITEMS

Historic Christian attitudes toward other communities varied a great deal depending on which community was involved, but the consequences of that fact need to be explored. We should expect Christian-Buddhist dialogue to be different from Christian-Muslim dialogue; likewise for Christian-Jewish and other conversations. It is important to observe this, since much of the literature on dialogue produced in the 1970s has been general and vague. By the 1980s, however, it became clearer that individual dialogue efforts would have to be more specific.

Christian-Hindu dialogue in India has found Indians receptive to Christian ideals of social betterment, indeed even expecting that contribution from Christianity. They have been less aware of the Christian spiritual traditions of contemplation and renunciation, despite efforts (notably by some French Catholic clergy in India) to live out these values in a Hindu society. Although educated Indians are usually more than willing to talk, many Hindus have not been as interested in dialogue as their Christian counter-parts. Excluding a few militant orthodox, Hindus typically are tolerant, but they do not have a specifically religious imperative for dialogue. Salvation is seen as the result of an individual's quest for liberation, not as the result of the preaching of a prophetic message. Moreover, as the over-whelming majority of Indians, Hindus see little pressure to relate corporately to the 2.5 percent of their society that is Christian. The fascination of Christianity for many Indians in fact is probably intellectual, because generations of British influence in their land have left a high regard for English literature and Western philosophy, both of which press certain questions of meaning and value onto the Indian consciousness in their Christian formulation. For Christians in a Hindu milieu, it is perhaps alternative modes of spiritual contemplation and ritual symbolism which may constitute the chief reward of dialogue.

It is similar with Buddhism. Buddhism is also a tradition which, on the whole, values liberation through individual insight more fundamentally than social change through prophetic preaching. While it is missionary in its outreach, it may be termed individualistic in the content of its specific message. Except for the Tibetan tradition (where the Dalai Lama is a very visible head), the Buddhist community does not have a centralized pattern of institu-tional and doctrinal authority as striking as Christianity's, particularly the Roman Catholic Church's. Hence we find the Buddhist fascination (or lack of it) with Christianity varying from one Buddhist land to another, reaching its peak perhaps most noticeably among Japanese intellectuals. Japanese universities, it should be noted, have academic departments of Buddhist philosophy and of Western philosophy as distinct and separate subjects. The challenge of Christianity to a Japanese Buddhist is not that of a domestic numerical minority but that of a powerful and tempting foreign intellectual influence. The appeal of Buddhism to the Christian, similarly, is both psychological and philosophical: Buddhism offers a contemplative discipline from which Christians may learn, and couples it with an analysis of the human personality which is fascinatingly different from Western notions of the self. In the long run, Christian-Buddhist dialogue, even when softened by East Asian styles of understatement in conversation, may be the most intellectually challenging of the various dialogues in which Christians are involved.

Christian-Islamic dialogue has probably undergone more change during the 1970s than any other area of interfaith dialogue. The change has not been one of substance, since the essential features of these two rival traditions remain unaltered. It has been a change of urgency and of attitude. During the 1970s, an increase in Muslims' national self-consciousness, highlighted by the 1979 revolution in Iran, made the world aware of Islamic traditionalism as a social and political force. Muslim-majority nations are now seen as acting not only out of secular national interests, but also for religious interests, sometimes at great sacrifice to a standard of living measured in Western economic or social terms. For the West, simply to understand such self-awareness is a pressing moral concern; and to remain in contact with the governments of all Islamic lands is a vital economic and political need. The surprising thing is that as the now "resurgent" Islamic world has gained political and economic power, many of its community leaders have become more

willing to talk, not less. One senses that Muslims now feel a
sense of dignity or pride in the presence of Westerners.
They know that, after centuries of Crusader polemic followed by centuries of patronizing colonial disdain, the
West is at last more willing to listen and to take Muslims
seriously as equals. It is therefore encouraging that, in
March 1982, for the first time, an international consultation
representing world Muslim and Christian organizations
called for the establishment of joint committees on matters
of mutual concern.

The initiatives for positive encounter between Muslims
and Christians have also grown out of needs in the local
society, in both the Islamic world and the West. Migration,
temporary or permanent, has brought Muslims to live in
Christian countries: Turks to West Germany, Algerians to
France, Pakistanis to Britain and Canada, Indonesians to
Holland, Arabs to the United States. Understanding one's
Muslim neighbors is no longer an international endeavor; it
goes on in many cities in the Christian world. When Islam
gets a bad press in our international news, the neighborly
task of building a sense of partnership is rendered more
difficult and more urgent.

Jews have often had mixed feelings about Christian-
Jewish dialogue. On the one hand, as a numerical minority,
they have felt it prudent to advance the wider community's
understanding of their heritage and their goals. On the
other, as recipients of centuries of pressure to conform,
convert, and assimilate, they have been suspicious that
dialogue is simply a new disguise for proselytizing. And
yet, individual Christian-Jewish friendships and conversations have flourished for generations, and it has been a
logical outgrowth of such conversations that encounters on
both practical and theoretical topics have been planned by
Jewish and Christian organizations.

Especially in academic circles, Christian-Jewish conversation has achieved some progress in looking historically at
the Jewish world in the time of the early church. The

Christian debt to Jewish scriptural and legal tradition has been explored, and the satisfactions of observing commandments, as in Psalm 119 and in Pharisaism, are more openly appreciated. Post-biblical Jewish thought, history, and devotion are still a closed book to far too many Christians, especially to those whose picture of biblical times tempts them to conclude that they have everything they need to know about Judaism.

In the decades since the end of World War II, two themes have dominated Christian-Jewish dialogue: the European holocaust and the contemporary State of Israel. These two are not separate but are rather intimately linked. As one rabbi put it to me, "We have a claim on you," meaning that because of what Christians did (or allowed others to do) in Europe from 1933 to 1945, Christians everywhere must now support Israel and its aims in the Middle East. Whether the Palestinian Arabs should have been required to pay the price for Hitler's atrocities against the Jews is one very debatable question, and whether Israel in its various wars against its neighbors has exceeded the minimum necessary for self-defense is another.

But it is indisputable that many Jewish leaders have treated critics of Israel's policies toward Arabs as harboring anti-Jewish hatred and wishing for a repeat of the evils of the holocaust. In the weeks after the Arab-Israeli "Six-Day War" of 1967, American Jewish leaders condemned the churches for "silence" on support for Israel, at a time when those same churches were vocally committed to seeking peace with justice and security for both Israelis and Arabs. A number of Jewish writers were particularly incensed that American blacks, whom Jews had supported on the domestic front in civil rights struggles, should now be calling for the support of the civil rights of Palestinians. Dialogue, the Jewish spokesmen said, was not possible unless Christians gave wholehearted support to Israel.

There exists among Christian denominations and councils a circle of people who have given their energy to

strengthening ties with the Jewish community and to com-
bating anti-Jewish prejudice. This group, which includes
people who worked in European refugee relief in the
1940s, is attentive and responsive to the claim made on
behalf of modern Israel. Another circle in the church world
includes people who have worked in Middle Eastern
refugee relief since the establishment of Israel, as well as
individuals involved in human rights and Third World
causes. This circle hears and responds to the Christian and
Muslim Palestinian call for justice.

In recent years there has been an encouraging sign: the
churches and church councils have been bringing their
responsibility and concern for each of these peoples more
frankly into their discussions. The emergence of trilateral
Christian-Jewish-Muslim dialogue has also been a hearten-
ing development. But it remains a delicate matter for the
Christian to communicate a universality of concern when
particular commitments have been at stake.

Christianity's need for dialogue in today's pluralistic
world is not merely bilateral, it is multilateral. Although
individual agenda items arise in particular bilateral situations, the Christian churches and councils in the world
today are carrying on many bilateral talks all at once. What
is more, this situation is more characteristic of Christianity
than of our various dialogue partners. Thanks to the acci-
dents of European exploration and technology, and of
colonial and missionary history, Western culture and Christian religion have circled the globe. Islam and Buddhism
are also worldwide missionary religions, but Christians
belong to the community that has the most geographically
widespread, and the most seriously developed, dialogue
with others. It is a major attainment, a daunting responsibility, and an exciting challenge.

5
THE TRUTH QUESTION

In John 18, Pilate asks Jesus whether he is the king of the Jews. Jesus answers that his kingdom is not of this world. When Pilate repeats the question, Jesus states that he has come into the world to bear witness to the truth. Pilate, clearly hesitant to convict on such testimony, asks, "What is truth?" The question goes unanswered, Pilate goes out to face the crowd, and John leaves his readers to their own conclusions. Presumably, the "truth" to which Jesus bears witness has to do with salvation offered by God. It is our task in this chapter to explore this and other understandings of religious truth.

SALVATION

"There is no salvation outside the church." More than any other phrase, this has represented for Catholics and for Protestants the "bottom line" of the church's teaching. When all is said and done, however much we may appreciate other people and their traditions, don't we have to claim that we have the inside track and the clearest path? Doesn't the church's stance require us to regard the doctrines of others as false (or at least as less than fully true) and their piety as mistaken (or at least as less effective in leading to salvation)? If things were otherwise, *how* could we, and *why* should we, proclaim the gospel?

The famous phrase comes from the early fathers of the church, such as Origen and Cyprian in the third century. When they used it, they were thinking of the confrontation with the pagan cults and philosophies of the Greek-speaking eastern Mediterranean. The phrase crops up again centuries later. In 1442 the Council of Florence reaffirmed and consolidated the position: no pagans, Jews, heretics, or schismatics can partake of eternal life. "Unless before the end of life they are joined to the church, they will go to the everlasting fire prepared for the devil and his angels." (Denzinger, *Enchiridion*, no. 714) In the years following that council, European Christianity struggled over the issues of the Protestant Reformation. The principal people the Catholic Church threatened with hellfire were the "schismatics," i.e., the Protestants. In later centuries the claim of a monopoly on salvation characterized Western Christians' missionary thinking about non-Christians.

What does the term "salvation" mean? The word itself is of Latin derivation, and had a pre-Christian secular meaning of health and safety as well as greeting. In Christian Latin the term was used to translate Hebrew notions of escape and deliverance, often from military peril, and to describe Hellenistic Greek notions of personal as well as political deliverance. It is possible that Christian usage was also influenced by Zoroastrian conceptions of Soshyant, a savior figure expected to set the cosmic order right. In any event, the New Testament epistles treat salvation as the believer's destiny obtained through Christ, and the Gospels marshal Jesus' birth narratives and the miracle stories to document the claim of his role and power as savior.

As Christianity dominated European thought for more than a millennium from Constantine to the Enlightenment, the dominant question was not how many paths to salvation there might be but how the Christian could travel the one

path. If one was to be saved, of course it would be salvation
through Christ. Included in the content of that salvation
might be a heavenly paradise rather than hell, an individual
victory over sin and evil, and a sense of vindication of
divine purpose in the history of the world.

The knowledge of other cultures and traditions that has
developed in modern times has pressed the term "salvation," with its background of specifically Christian mean-
ings, into use as a description of other religions as well. In
the comparative study of religion, the mystery cults of the
Greek and Roman world have been termed "salvation
religions," and the Hindu term for release, *moksha*, has
been translated by some as salvation. Simply observing
religion as a phenomenon, one can see that what the
Christian calls salvation is like what various religious
traditions offer to their followers. There are many pitfalls in
identifying something in another tradition by a word so rich
in Christian connotations, but the fact is that some observ-
ers have been making such an identification.

So much for the descriptive study of religions, but what
about theology? Can a theologian reasoning from a stand-
point of faith make room for salvation outside the church?
Many Protestants and Catholics in modern times have said
no, agreeing in effect with the Council of Florence. God has
the power to save anyone, but he has simply chosen some
(i.e., us) and not others. Others, however, particularly in
Catholic theology, have held that God wills the salvation of
all people, and that through God's grace he is already
reaching out to the non-Christian. Furthermore, since
God's grace is mediated through Jesus Christ—almost by
definition, as it were—the non-Christian is saved in Christ
even if he has never heard the name of Christ. Do not
expect a non-Christian to confirm such a statement from his
own point of view; to affirm this position depends on a
certain prior investment in the Christian tradition.

THEORIES OF TRUTH

There are different ways in which truth can be understood and confirmed, and these have been described in various philosophical traditions.

1. *Propositional truth.* In many ways the simplest and most direct view of truth, this theory holds that Christian faith-statements are cognitive and factual, and may be corroborated by reference to recognized authority. God is a "fact." So is revelation, God's incarnation in Jesus Christ, Jesus' resurrection, God's redemption of the world through his suffering and death, and so on. Therefore, Christianity is true when it makes certain statements about human nature and experience. Other religions, which make conflicting statements, are mistaken. Islam, for instance, is in error when the Qur'an states that God did not beget and was not begotten; or Hinduism, in holding that divinity has become incarnate on multiple occasions.

Others hold that the notion of Christian truth, while factual, is true symbolically or metaphorically. "God" may not be quite the personal, even anthropomorphic, figure the Bible at points pictures him to be; he may be the guiding principle of the universe; incarnation in Jesus may be a manner of saying that Jesus exemplifies his will, and so on. But treating some or all of the Christian faith-statements as symbolic does not necessarily alter the stance toward the claims of other religions. One could still hold, if one wished, that Christianity correctly symbolizes God, human nature, and the universe, whereas another religion does not.

2. *Coherent truth.* Another view holds that Christianity is cognitively true but establishes its truth on a different basis. Rather than seeking to show correspondence to an external event or authority, a "coherence" theory of truth sees the Christian faith as a system. Its references are

internal, within a kind of closed circle. There are at least
two levels at which such a circle can be described. One is
the circularity of argument: Christian statements can depend philosophically on their own conclusions. The God
Jesus reveals, for example, must be the sort of God who
would reveal himself in Jesus. Or the God whom Jesus
reveals must be one of such grace as to have revealed
himself through Jesus to all humanity, pre-Christian and
post-Christian pagans included. Another level is the nature
of the Christian community as a circle: Christian statements, while not necessarily "factual" even when taken
symbolically, "make sense" in the light of the tradition that
produced them. Many of us indulge in such an attitude
when we sing hymns which we would hesitate to pro-
nounce as propositional creeds.

The coherence view of truth can admit the possibility
that there may be other self-contained systems, equally
self-consistent and possibly equally valid, in the other
religions of the world. A Christian claim that Christianity
makes coherent logical sense may mean that any other
systematic tradition has the right to be similarly "true."

3. *Developmental truth.* Rather than representing God
as Being, some positions speak of Becoming. God is not so
much Fact as he is Goal. Religious institutions and ideas
represent developing stages of human progress or awareness.

Christianity sees itself in this historical relationship with
its predecessor, ancient Judaism. But to represent the
newer as the truer revelation is a risky business: how does
the Christian handle Islam? Christians who wanted to think
developmentally in this way regarded Islam as a devolu-
tion, a heretical falling away from the sequence of valid
prophets or covenants. Such views of Islam have more
recently been seen as unreasonable and indefensible.

During the late nineteenth century, anthropologists and
other social scientists, influenced by Darwin's discovery of
biological evolution, generated many theories of the evolu-

tion of religion. They hoped that by reconstructing its prehistoric origin, through supposed parallels with surviving tribal religions, they could explain its essential nature. In the social sciences such theories of origins went out of fashion after World War I, giving way to nondevelopmental theories of the contemporary function of religion in particular societies. But among Christian apologists a notion of Christianity as a sequential fulfillment of the aspirations of other religions has persisted.

4. *Pragmatic truth.* "The proof of the pudding is in the eating," the proverb goes; or, in Jesus' words, "By their fruits you shall know them." One test of any religion is what kind of results it produces. If Christianity makes people better people, what better could be said for it?

Some may argue that this position shifts the agenda from fact to value, and that we have no business mixing up facts and values. Semantically, the word "valid" clearly spans both the notion of argument and the notion of worthwhileness. More important is the very strong Christian association of truth and goodness throughout the two thousand years of our tradition. To be a "true" Christian is to follow the commandments of God as Father and to act in "imitation" of Christ. One of the central truths of Christianity has often been held to be Jesus' insight into human nature as shown most notably in the parables and in the Sermon on the Mount. What *was* the "truth" to which Jesus bore witness when he stood before Pilate in John 18? A truth of moral action, many would argue.

Where does this put other religions? They must be true to the extent that their moral and ritual conduct produces benefits for their adherents comparable to those of Christianity. How do we judge? Apparently, we should be able to assess social benefit far more conclusively than something like the coherence of symbolic statements. Yet we have already seen that it is treacherous to confuse the ideals and the achievements of religions. Are we really content that *our* religion's ideals should be judged by *our* sporadic

fidelity to them? How then dare we judge the "truth" of
another religion by the limits of its adherents' accomplishments? What's sauce for the goose is sauce for the gander.

Still, the notion of "truth" as action deserves attention. A
passage in John 14, one of the principal proof texts used for
Christian exclusivism, reads, "I am the way, and the truth,
and the life; no one comes to the Father, but by me." Notice
that the word "truth" is sandwiched between "way" and
"life." Far from being a repudiation of other religions as
teachings, this passage can be taken as promoting Christ-
like action as the criterion of faithfulness.

5. *Existential truth.* One of the most persuasive and
widespread modern approaches to religious truth holds that
religious affirmations are not statements of outward fact but
refer to the experience, attitude, or commitment of the
believer. Religious statements, like statements of love, are
not externally verifiable but rather take their truth from the
integrity and commitment of whoever makes them. Some
such statements, when cast in the form of declarations or
promises, depend for their validity partly on whether the
speaker or writer who made them has the capability to carry
them out.

When we are talking about this kind of truth we are
talking a language of commitment and of participation. The
truth of Christianity is not something we can point to "out
there" as though it were a mathematical theorem. It is
something we recognize by living the life of Christian
commitment: we experience the truth of Christianity; it
becomes true *for us;* one can even say we make it true.
Faith, understood as commitment regarding something that
is unprovable but also un*dis*provable, continues to have an
intellectually respectable sphere in which to operate.

Critics of an existentialist position may want to reduce it
to a mere "I believe because I believe," and continue to
seek some elusive external proof for religion. The existentialist view, however, does take account of the demonstra-
ble fact of religious commitment on the part of many who

contend that, in effect, experience is its own proof. It takes account of the human fact of the particularity of heritage and experience and loyalty.

My tradition is something for which I cherish an affection, and I would not suddenly discard it the way I would throw away last year's telephone directory when the new one comes out. I was born and raised an American Presbyterian, and Presbyterian lore has a fascination for me which cannot be explained on rational grounds. I have also struggled with my heritage, particularly the grim details of a Calvinist understanding of predestination. I have come to terms with predestination by understanding the doctrine historically to have developed from a desire, which I share, to stress God's sovereignty, rather than from a desire to consign newborn infants to damnation, which I doubt ever gave positive satisfaction to many Calvinists. Having struggled thus, I observe and appreciate that others struggle with their heritages too: the Jew or the Muslim seeking to understand the goodness of God in the events of history, or the Hindu or Buddhist seeking to find meaning in suffering.

Consider an analogy. My tradition is like my family's snapshots, yours like your family's. My album does not have an "objective" market value, but a unique personal one. I might try to rescue photographs rather than appliances if the house were on fire. Because of the value I experience in my heritage, I can appreciate the way you might value yours. Christian faith may thus be the soundest basis for an appreciation of the faith of others; as Christianity is true in our experience, we can for instance accept and appreciate how Hinduism might be true for a Hindu.

The criticism one must meet in order to maintain a position like this is a cluster of problems that can be called relativism. In terms of information or doctrinal clarity, are not some religions more true than others? For example, most of us would put Confucianism ahead of Shinto in this respect. In terms of social value, are not some religions more true than others? Hardly anyone would want to put

the Quakers and the Jonestown cult on the same level.
Religions are to be appreciated because of people's commitment to them, but an existentialist theology of religions
is likely to introduce a judgment of validity about the
"object" or referent of that commitment.

In *Christianity and the Encounter of the World Religions*
(1963; p. 79), Paul Tillich asked where Christianity finds its
criteria. The only point from which the criteria can be
derived, through participation in its continuing spiritual
power, is "the event on which Christianity is based," "the
appearance and reception of Jesus of Nazareth as the
Christ, a symbol which stands for the decisive self-manifes-
tation in human history of the source and aim of all being."

Tillich was content to interpret the power of the universe
through the events and vocabulary of the Christian tradition. Late in his career he lectured in Japan, talked with
Buddhists, and began to feel the need to rework and restate
his thought in more pluralistic or universal terms. A position like Tillich's, which starts from one's own tradition and
experience and takes account of others' by analogy, may yet
be the shape of Christian theology in the decades to come.
But such a position will be under pressure to specify
criteria for identifying a pattern of allegiance as a "religion"
and for considering it valid or true. Christians who use
traditional Christian standards for judging other religions
will at least be able to say with integrity that the standards
are their own, but they may be cautioned in dialogue not to
impose them on others.

6. *Truth as beyond determination.* We are accustomed to
thinking of God as a being or power who transcends the
finite world. Analogously, one might argue for a theory of
religious truth which transcends the finiteness of our ability
to think in concepts.

It has long been a technique of religious reasoning not to
limit God by saying that God has a particular specific
characteristic; instead, one leaves God's nature more un-
specified by saying that he is not described by some

characteristic. This pattern of reasoning is called the *via negativa,* or "negative way," in theology. It is found in various religions. A famous passage in the Hindu Brihad-Aranyaka Upanishad, for example, says that Brahman (the world-soul) is not to be equated with this and not with that. The *via negativa* has been a particularly common approach among writers describing mystical or contemplative experiences: experiencing God, or the absolute, represents some way of going beyond ordinary forms.

It is not a large step from the position that God goes beyond the limits of description in language to the position that religious truth goes beyond the limits of conceptual thought. As the world must not be thought of as limiting God, so thought itself must not be thought of as limiting truth. We are led to a truth which is ineffable (inexpressible): not ineffable in practice because we have not yet found the precise terms or the right analogy in which it is to be stated, but ineffable in principle as beyond all statements. This notion regards truth as a quality of the Absolute, beyond the particulars of religion. A religion may point or lead toward truth, but truth cannot be confined, contained, or exhausted by any religious form, system, or concept.

A notion that truth transcends conceptualization is found in Western religions especially among their mystics—those who have reported and reflected on an intense experience of oneness with God. Mysticism appears as a movement in medieval Judaism, Christianity, and Islam. By analogy, we label certain South and East Asian religious philosophies mystical as well. Some Hindus stressed the oneness of the self with the universe as an intellectual reality that could be felt experientially. Likewise, philosophical Taoism talks of the Way that is beyond and behind the flux of everyday events. But it is probably Mahayana Buddhist thought, beginning with Nagarjuna about A.D. 200 and developing in the Chinese T'ien-t'ai and Hua-yen schools thereafter, that brought the topic closest to the center of the stage. The

Buddhists spoke of the three "bodies" of the Buddha, of which the *dharma*-body or Buddha-nature was understood as truth, in the sense of being this inexpressible Absolute beyond all the impermanence of manifestations and finiteness of conceptualizations.

The notion of truth as Absolute is one which has appeared in various traditions. It says that the religious traditions are not truth in themselves, but that truth is beyond them. A Christian who takes such a position will say that Christianity points to the truth. A Christian will certainly not say that Christianity has the whole truth, for there will be no way of demonstrating that other traditions cannot also point toward truth.

TRUTH AND LOVE

This review of theories of truth has not resolved the nature of truth at all. Rather, it has opened the question even wider. Today we do not need to close off various options affecting the Christian relationship to other religions but must try to explore a number of them as sensitively and openly as possible. If we are aware that Christianity has not spoken with one voice across the centuries about the nature of its claim to truth, and that Christians do not do so today, we will be more responsible partners in the current dialogue.

The search for truth, understood in doctrinal terms, has always been highly valued in the Christian tradition—more so than in a number of other religions. Yet true belief is not the sole concern of Christian commitment or the defining characteristic of Christian identity. The Gospel authors said, "Believe," but they also report Jesus as saying, "Love." The core of Christian identity lays on us an obligation to love our neighbor—including our non-Christian neighbor—that must be weighed against the obligation to assert the truth of our creed. What, then, if our insistence

on preaching our belief is an offense to the integrity and
identity of our non-Christian neighbor? Christ's commandment to love that neighbor may imply that we curtail our
insistence on our own rightness. Put simply, to tell the
Hindu, for example, that he cannot find salvation or fulfillment in his own tradition and community is morally a very
un-Christian thing to do.

The recognition of this point is not new. It has been
around for at least the half century since Hocking's commission questioned the effectiveness and rationale of Christian
missions. It was well stated in 1960 by E. L. Allen in
Christianity Among the Religions: "The Christian is under
two obligations in this matter, one to truth and one to love,
and these have equal claim upon him. On the one hand he
must stand by that which convinces him of his truth. . . . On
the other hand, he will look with charity, as on all men, so
on all manifestations of the spiritual life" (p. 119).

Wilfred Cantwell Smith has argued for an appreciation of
the faith of other persons as persons. He charges the
Christian West with arrogance in its historic approach to
Asia and Africa. In a lecture in 1961 he said: "It is far too
sweeping to condemn the great majority of mankind to lives
of utter meaninglessness and perhaps to hell, simply on the
basis of what seems to some individuals the force of logic.
. . . The damnation of my neighbour is too weighty a matter
to rest on a syllogism" ("Christianity in a Religiously Plural
World," in *Religious Diversity,* 1976).

These are strong and challenging words. There may be a
temptation, among those who agree with them, to meet the
vocal objections of some of our dialogue partners by water-
ing down the content of Christian assertions. Maybe we
should not say that the church is sole heir to the promises to
Israel, or maybe faith in Christ is not the only means by
which God saves people, even anonymously. Perhaps a
better way to tone down what has been perceived as
arrogance is not to change the content of the Christian claim

but to change the manner of its proclamation. When we
make statements that are exclusive, let us make it clear that
the exclusiveness is seen from the viewpoint of participation in our own community.

With those of other communities we share a common
humanity. Our "world" and the "world" of others is located
on this one planet. What differentiates "our world" from the
world of another community is the particular, historically
defined perspective from which we see the one world.

We should not sacrifice our commitment to truth in the
name of a bland intercommunal love. Truth is an obligation,
as is love. Our task is to bear honest witness to our vision of
truth, but to do so in a humble way, always open to the
discovery of others' insights.

THE UNITY OF RELIGIONS?

I am attending a conference in another city, enroute from
the airport to the convention hotel in a taxi. The driver asks
where I'm from and what my line of work is, and I respond
that I'm in the comparative study of religion. He opens up:
"Say, I've been meaning to ask somebody a question. The
religions are all the same, aren't they?" Professors give
fifty-minute lectures in response to questions such as that. I
can count on only five minutes with the driver—fortunately
for him. What am I to say? The honest answer, of course, is
that there are similarities and there are also differences.
Individual judgment will have to determine how much
importance to attach to each. I will probably learn more
than the driver during the ride, for I will find out what he
considers to be the essential shared feature prompting his
question.

But the significant thing about such conversations—and
I've experienced them frequently enough for them to form
a pattern—is that they are evidence of a widely held view
among people in many walks of life. Theologians, and

theological curricula, have devoted little time to the similarity of religions. When one knows only one tradition well, the topic usually does not arise. The average person in the street, especially our philosopher behind the taxi wheel, may know about several traditions more or less equally, even if not that well. Popular awareness of religions is general; it is also sketchy and its definitions are often imprecise. When the theologians emerge from their studies, however, this is the simple social fact they have to face.

Up to a point, our driver's question is simply evidence of the pluralism in our society: various religions exist, and have an equal right to exist. But note that our driver has implied far more: they also have equal content and equal truth. Is he correct? To answer properly, we would need quantities of survey information on the world religions, but we will also have to clarify certain problems of comparison.

One such problem is how to decide when a parallel exists at all. Does a certain feature found in more than one religion—sprinkling with water, let us say—have a constant meaning? Water can cleanse, as in Christian baptism and Zoroastrian purification ritual, but sprinkling water can also be an attempt to bring rain. More similarity of detail would help us to demonstrate a parallel. A perceptive empathy helps too, as in the work of Mircea Eliade; he cuts across tribal religions and world religions, noting similarities as manifestations of a general human sense of the sacred.

Historians need to decide a related issue: when does a parallel prove an influence? Mere similarity of basic life experiences may not be enough, such as the association of light with good and darkness with evil; but convincing instances of similarity through shared heritage abound. The biblical story of Noah and the flood clearly comes from a Mesopotamian epic. Psalm 29 appears to be an adaptation of a Canaanite hymn to Baal. The halo may have spread from Sasanian Iran in the third to seventh centuries A.D., where it associated the king's glory with the radiant disk of the sun, to Europe, in medieval Christian art, and to China, in medieval Buddhist art. People from the Buddhist world to the Islamic to the Christian all use rosaries as an aid to devotion, possibly through geographic spread. More tantalizing still is the suggestion that the Christian monastic tradition was patterned after Buddhist asceticism in the early Christian centuries, but we lack the documents to demonstrate this.

To talk of the unity of religions, therefore, may include their similarity in form but also their historical interrelatedness. Such talk tends to treat shared features as essential while treating distinctive features as incidental. We must thus be careful not to overlook fundamental differences but must seek to understand them. One example will have to suffice. A leading Toronto rabbi stated in a dialogue that the Christian ideal of forgiveness was an absurdly impossible expectation of people; I am obliged to strive to appreciate why he might say so. And yet the inscription "Father forgive" behind the altar in the bombed-out shell of Coventry cathedral is one of the most compelling and moving (one of the truest?) sights I have ever seen. That Coventry has become a sort of penitential pilgrimage site for German visitors to England suggests that I am not alone in such a feeling, nor is the ideal necessarily absurd.

To talk of similarities and influences and borrowings can be disquieting to some traditional theologians. Borrowings militate against the idea of a tradition growing up in either blissful isolation from, or radical rejection of, its neighbors. To condemn borrowings, theologians have frequently used the term "syncretism," a word of Greek derivation. Syncretism denotes a combination of practices from different religions; but beyond that, it connotes a judgment that the mixture is illegitimate. People charged with syncretism are often charged with "selling out." In accepting borrowed contaminants consciously or unconsciously, they are polluting the purity of the normative faith.

The charge of syncretism is frequently made by a community on the defensive. For religious traditions have borrowed in the past, and in today's interconnected world they can hardly avoid influencing each other. In times of vitality and confidence, communities have borrowed quite freely what was useful to them, provided that they could satisfy themselves that it was in keeping with their own central standards and affirmations. Descriptively, the religions have much in common, and I could even suggest to my taxi driver that they will have more in common in the future.

It is interesting, therefore, to see certain writers making a virtue of necessity by trying to rehabilitate the connotations of the word "syncretism." The German Protestant theologian Jürgen Moltmann does so, for example. The other religions, Moltmann holds, are "provisional," and Christianity, which is absolute, can take over from them what it finds to be good, true, and beautiful. In *The Church in the Power of the Spirit* (1977) Moltmann writes, "It is precisely because of its syncretistic openness that the Christian religion is to excel all others, so proving itself the absolute religion." Frankly, I am uncomfortable with talk of Christianity or any religion as absolute. Religions are relative; God is absolute.

A crucial question on syncretism is whether the traffic of influences is one-way. Moltmann next speaks of Christianity as a "critical catalyst," using a phrase from his Tübingen colleague Hans Küng. The presence of Christians in the environment of other communities, Moltmann and Küng both claim, infuses certain ideas into the internal development of those traditions. Both Moltmann and Küng note the influence of Christianity on the other religions; but both go on to suggest that Christianity itself will be reciprocally influenced as well: "a Christianity tinged with different religions" (Moltmann), a spirit of open-mindedness "which destroys nothing of value in the religions, but also does not incorporate uncritically anything worthless" (Küng).

Inevitably, the quest for the theological meaning of other religions means broadening the traditional sense of, and search for, religious truth. As such a quest unfolds, the truth to which we can hope to bear witness will build on, but will be greater than, the truth we now know.

6
WHAT FUTURE?

Even in bygone days, religions did not remain static. What they were at any given moment was the product of prior changes and influences. Today, nobody needs to be told that we are living in a time of accelerating change. What the future of religions will be within our own lifetime, let alone later on, is hard to predict.

Some societies, particularly Marxist ones, have thought it possible to do without religion. Religion, Karl Marx said using a phrase from Charles Kingsley, is the "opium of the masses." Supposedly, humanity can kick the habit: religion can be abandoned by people and societies that take control of their own destiny into their own hands. In communist states like the Soviet Union and China, religious institutions have been subjected to a generation of control and repression. Though weakened, they survive, and show no sign of disappearing altogether overnight. Religion linked to an ethnic base, particularly in the Muslim minorities of Soviet and Chinese Central Asia, has a special tenacity. But the transmission of religion within the family, especially from baby-sitting grandparent to grandchild, cannot be overlooked.

My experience teaching in a world religions institute in China attests that while religious institutions in the People's Republic are weak, religious curiosity is strong. The questions of meaning and value which religions ask and

answer are universal questions arising from our common
human situation. What is the meaning of life? Is there
power or purpose in control of the world? Why do evil acts
go unpunished? What happens after I die? No matter how
weak religious institutions may become, religious questions will persist.

At the social level, pluralism in Western society has
become an undisputed fact. However, in their expression of
group identity and intellectual or doctrinal tradition, many
religious communities still have to come to terms with
today's facts. The central problem of this book—how to
make room in a community's self-understanding for the
insights and self-understanding of others—remains a problem for other groups as well as our own.

I believe that one of the ways we will handle this will be
with an awareness that our own tradition, like other people's traditions, is part of a historical and cultural context. It
involves a kind of critical distance from one's own tradition,
an ability to see ourselves as others see us and as we see
them. It involves seeing our tradition as having developed,
rather than being absolute; seeing it as having developed,
as others have developed; seeing it as open to further
development. Whether traditionalists like it or not, this
critical awareness increasingly characterizes the students I
see in the university. The same awareness will characterize
the people who attend worship in Christian churches in the
future. A naive or heavy-handed insistence from the pulpit
that Christianity has an exclusive monopoly on truth will
cause intelligent people in the pews to look elsewhere for
guidance.

"By their fruits you shall know them." The real test of the
religions, ours included—the real test of their approach to
each other—is whether they will actually do anything to
improve the world we live in. A theoretical appreciation of
the doctrine or ritual of another community counts for very
little if we do not also urgently address ourselves to the
needs of humanity at large. There is too much suffering and

110

starvation in the world, too many destitute refugees, too much prejudice and hatred, too much waste of precious resources.

Contemplation may have its place in religion, but mere contemplation is a luxury. Jesus, contemplating Jerusalem on Palm Sunday in Luke 19, weeps for the anguish of humanity. Were he to return today to Jerusalem (or Beirut, or Dresden, or Hiroshima) he would find that nineteen centuries have done little to improve humanity's performance. An unfinished human agenda confronts the religions.

I must close on a personal note. The comparative study of the world's religions has been my professional life for nearly two decades, and an intellectual interest for closer to three. During that time I have been privileged to know authoritative scholarly adherents of several major traditions and also to have information from authoritative "outside" and "critical" sources. I have lived more than two years in West Asia, a year in South Asia, and half a year in East Asia. Besides reading about Asian traditions, I have joined prayer in their temples and mosques, breathed their incense, contemplated their art, shared their food, listened to their music and their silence, and pursued conversations late into the night about the meaning of life and death. I have removed my shoes, knelt, chanted, and lit candles. To share the life and worship of another community is an opportunity I would wish for every reader of this book.

At no time have I ever thought of myself as anything other than a Christian. At no time have I ever supposed that God could not adequately reach out to me, to challenge and to comfort, in my own Christian faith and community. Yet at no time have I ever supposed that God could not also reach out to other persons in their traditions and communities as fully and as satisfyingly as he has to me in mine. At no time have I ever felt I would be justified in seeking to uproot an adherent of another tradition from his faithful following of that tradition. My Christianity—including my sense of

Christian ministry—has commanded that I be open to learn from the faith of others.

What, then, is the meaning of others' faith, and of other faiths? If God is the loving Spirit and power that Christ has shown us he is, we cannot imagine him forsaking the adherents of other religions. We trust God will lead them and us into a new awareness of full partnership and community, with a mutually agreed sense of purpose to face the world's many tasks. To rearrange some phrases from Eph. 3:20, the church in years to come will more fully glorify Christ Jesus to the extent that it worships God as one who is able to do far more abundantly than all that we have hitherto asked or thought.

QUESTIONS FOR STUDY AND DISCUSSION

Chapter 1. STARTING WITH THE BIBLE

1. What might Judaism have been like if the Babylonians had not conquered Jerusalem, destroyed the Temple, and deported Israel's leaders?

2. First read Isaiah 8 as a short-range political prediction, and next read Isaiah 7. Then give a Jewish critique of the traditional Christian interpretation of Isa. 7:14.

3. Which individuals did Jesus accept and which did he not, and on what criteria?

4. If you were a Jew in first-century Jerusalem, would you support armed rebellion against the Roman government? Why?

Chapter 2. THE CHURCH'S CLASSIC POSITION

1. In Acts 19, how seriously interested is Paul in the philosophical traditions of the people of Ephesus?

2. In Acts 17, is Paul claiming that the "unknown god" he now preaches conforms to what the Athenians expected of God, or is he claiming that God is significantly different? Give reasons for your answer.

3. Read Acts 4 and notice the wonder-working activities of the Christian apostles. In this context, what alternatives did Peter have in mind when he said "there is no other

name" by which we are saved?

4. What effect did the discovery of the Americas in the fifteenth century have on Christian thinking about religions?

5. What would someone mean who refers to the American way of life as a "religion"?

Chapter 3. PLURALISM AND EVANGELISM

1. In publicly supported schools, what are the arguments for and against rotating interdenominational and interfaith prayer instead of no formal prayer at all?

2. What should parents do if a college-age son or daughter becomes involved with the Unification Church while exhibiting a marked change in communicativeness and behavior?

3. Evaluate proposed legislation to regulate the preaching activities of all, or some, religious groups.

4. What justification do Jehovah's Witnesses give for going from door to door in their evangelistic efforts?

5. What advice should be given to an African convert from tribal religion to Christianity who has two wives, in view of the church's teaching on monogamy and divorce?

6. If you had been pope, which side would you have supported in the Chinese Rites Controversy? What reasons would you have given for your stand?

Chapter 4. GROUND RULES FOR DIALOGUE

1. Would you call the piety of a Hindu worshiping before an image of Shiva "idolatry"? How would you explain your characterization?

2. When there are no adherents of a religion left, as with the followers of Baal or Apollo, what has the notion of dialogue to contribute to our understanding of them?

3. On what grounds can one claim that Hinduism is more tolerant than Christianity?

4. Why is the Bible a difficult starting place for discussion in Christian-Jewish dialogue?

5. Pakistan and Israel were both created as modern states in which one religious community could predominate. What are the costs and the benefits of such states in a pluralistic age?

Chapter 5. THE TRUTH QUESTION

1. What effect did the discovery of biological evolution have on modern theories of the nature of religion?

2. What does it mean to say that the parable of the good Samaritan, presumably not an account of a historical event, is "true"?

3. What is meant by reference to a universal human quality called "religiousness" or "faith"?

4. Hanukkah was a quite minor festival in the Jewish religious year for nineteen centuries. Discuss the claim that recent American Jewish attention to it, since it comes at the Christmas season, is an example of "syncretism."

5. If someone referred to your religious statements as "symbolic," what would this mean?

Chapter 6. WHAT FUTURE?

1. Why would anyone think there is a problem with the statement "I happen to be Christian"?

2. How do you think the pattern of participation in, or identification with, religious traditions in our society will be different twenty or thirty years from now, as compared with today?

3. What, specifically, can an individual Christian do to promote peace in the world?

4. If you see your own religion as the product of specific

historical and cultural contexts, and if you grant others in their contexts an equal right to their tradition, how do you meet the objection that your position is relativistic?

5. What criteria or what procedure can be set forth to decide whether someone has understood a religious tradition other than his or her own?

FOR FURTHER READING

Of the many writings that attempt to cover the whole range of our topic the classic in my view is by the philosopher E. L. Allen, *Christianity Among the Religions* (London: Allen & Unwin, 1960). It is historically literate, philosophically perceptive, and openly sympathetic to the riches of other traditions. That no book has surpassed it in more than twenty years as the subject has come closer to the center of theological attention is evidence that Allen writes well and that he contributes worthwhile considerations.

To locate studies of specific religious traditions, an indispensable reference work is the volume of bibliographical essays edited by Charles J. Adams, *A Reader's Guide to the Great Religions*, 2d ed. (Free Press, 1976).

On biblical topics the beginner should not overlook such references as *The Interpreter's Dictionary of the Bible* (Abingdon Press, 1962–76). Its article on "Nations," however, is not as useful as the book by Robert Martin-Achard, *A Light to the Nations* (Edinburgh: Oliver & Boyd, 1962). A provocative work on the impact of the Jewish war with Rome and the differentiation of the Christians from Judaism is S. G. F. Brandon, *The Fall of Jerusalem and the Christian Church*, 2d ed. (London: S.P.C.K., 1957). Specific biblical passages recurring in today's theological discussions are studied by Kenneth Cracknell in *Why Dialogue? A First British Comment on the W.C.C. Guidelines* (London: British Council of Churches, 1980).

Owen Thomas, *Attitudes Toward Other Religions* (Harper & Row, 1969), introduces an anthology of passages from key theologians with, among other things, a good typology of classic Christian views on the topic. Another typology, with reactions to the positions sketched, is in Charles Davis, *Christ and the World Religions* (London: Hodder & Stoughton, 1970). Another useful anthology, but without introductions, is *Christianity and Other Religions: Selected Readings*, edited by John Hick and Brian Hebblethwaite (Glasgow: William Collins Sons & Co., 1980). On the Roman Catholic Church's position on the necessity of the church for salvation, see articles in the *New Catholic Encyclopedia* (McGraw-Hill Book Co., 1967) and *Sacramentum Mundi* (London: Burns & Oates, 1969). Also useful is part A/III of Hans Küng, *On Being a Christian* (Doubleday & Co., 1976), and part G/I of Küng, *Does God Exist?* (Doubleday & Co., 1980).

The accumulation of information about other religions, part of the background of pluralism, is well traced by Eric J. Sharpe, *Comparative Religion: A History* (London: Gerald Duckworth & Co., 1975). The classic statement of the social fact of American pluralism was Will Herberg, *Protestant— Catholic—Jew* (Doubleday & Co., 1955). More recent theological responses include the conference papers edited by Gerald H. Anderson and Thomas F. Stransky, *Christ's Lordship and Religious Pluralism* (Orbis Books, 1981).

To mention Kenneth Scott Latourette's seven-volume *A History of the Expansion of Christianity* (Harper & Brothers, 1937–45) is not to denigrate more recent surveys such as Stephen Neill, *Christian Missions* (Harmondsworth: Penguin Books, 1964), or many specific studies such as John K. Fairbank, ed., *The Missionary Enterprise in China and America* (Harvard University Press, 1974). William E. Hocking, *Re-thinking Missions: A Laymen's Inquiry After One Hundred Years* (Harper & Brothers, 1932), and Hendrik Kraemer, *The Christian Message in a Non-Christian World* (London: Edinburgh House Press, 1938), outline a classic debate. More recent mission thinking is reflected in Gerald H. Anderson, ed., *The Theology of the Christian Mission* (McGraw-Hill Book Co., 1961), and a provocative challenge is Wilfred Cantwell Smith's chapter "Participation: The Changing Christian Role in Other Cultures," in his *Religious Diversity* (Harper & Row, 1976).

I must confess a certain frustration with much of the literature on interreligious dialogue. The pamphlet *Guidelines for Dialogue with People of Living Faiths and Ideologies* (Geneva: World Council of Churches, 1979) is fine as far as it goes but is neither theoretical nor systematic. An authoritative historical study of the developing emphasis on dialogue, however, is Carl F. Hallencreutz, *Dialogue and Community: Ecumenical Issues in Inter-religious Relationships* (Uppsala and Geneva: Swedish Institute of Missionary Research and World Council of Churches, 1977). A discerning guide to subsequent discussions is Kenneth Cracknell, *Considering Dialogue* (London: British Council of Churches, 1981). Still valuable for substantive reflection on the meaning and the potential of dialogue is Herbert Jai Singh, ed., *Inter-Religious Dialogue* (Bangalore: Christian Institute for the Study of Religion and Society, 1967). Another good anthology is Richard W. Rousseau, ed., *Interreligious Dialogue: Facing the Next Frontier* (Ridge Row Press, 1981). Anyone entering into dialogue should read the views of others as anthologized by David W. McKain, ed., *Christianity: Some Non-Christian Appraisals* (McGraw-Hill Book Co., 1964). Ninian Smart's book *A Dialogue of Religions* (London: SCM Press, 1960), rather than being about the activity of dialogue, is cast in dialogue form, its characters representing philosophical positions as conceived by the author.

Some books on Christian encounter with particular religious traditions narrate it in personal terms. a good example is Klaus Klostermaier, *In the Paradise of Krishna* (Westminster Press, 1971). Other books are more historical or analytical. Laudable because of its hope for a three-way dialogue, though brief, is James Kritzeck, *Sons of Abraham: Jews, Christians and Moslems* (Helicon Press, 1965). Three good examples of Christian intellectual encounter with Asian traditions are Heinrich Dumoulin, *Christianity Meets Buddhism* (Open Court Publishing Co., 1974); Julia Ching, *Confucianism and Christianity: A Comparative Study* (Tokyo: Kodansha, 1977); and Kenneth Cragg, *The Call of the Minaret* (Oxford University Press, 1956).

The British philosopher and theologian John H. Hick has gathered a number of his articles under the title *God Has Many Names* (Westminster Press, 1982). These span his own experience of broadened horizons, the questions of other religions' access to God and the comparability of religious experience, and the role of dialogue in an age of pluralism. For anyone interested in systematic and philosophical implications of our topic, this book is particularly appropriate.

The truth question crops up implicitly or explicitly in much of the literature already mentioned, but also in the discussion edited by John H. Hick, *Truth and Dialogue in World Religions* (Westminster Press, 1974). Philosophically rigorous, restricted to the form and status of statements, is William A. Christian, *Oppositions of Religious Doctrines: A Study in the Logic of Dialogue Among Religions* (London: Macmillan Publishers, 1972). An excitingly innovative and comprehensive fourfold typology of the relations between the enterprise of philosophy and that of religion is Max J. Charlesworth, *Philosophy of Religion: The Historic Approaches* (London: Macmillan Publishers, 1972). Some of the basic perennial questions are put succinctly and engagingly in "A Final Examination," the concluding pages of Huston Smith's readable survey *The Religions of Man* (Harper & Brothers, 1957), a widely used introductory text for over a quarter century, whose sympathy for East Asian religions has proved contagious. The use of Huston Smith's book by millions of people, indeed, is part of the phenomenon we have been considering: the new openness toward others in our times.